D1519438

MIND
AND
MOOD

ROBERT H. CURTIS, M.D.

MIND AND MOOD

UNDERSTANDING AND CONTROLLING YOUR EMOTIONS

Charles Scribner's Sons • New York

To Jeremy with love

Illustration on page 23 is from *Human Anatomy and Physiology*, by Alexander P. Spence and Elliot B. Mason, copyright © 1983, 1979 by The Benjamin/Cummings Publishing Co., Inc. Reprinted by permission.

ACKNOWLEDGMENT

The author is deeply grateful to John J. Piel, M.D., one of the pioneers of adolescent medicine, for his kindness in reviewing the manuscript and for his many excellent suggestions.

Library of Congress Cataloging-in-Publication Data
Curtis, Robert H.   Mind and mood.
Bibliography: p.   Includes index.
1. Emotions.   2. Emotions—Psychological effect.
3. Adolescent psychology.   I. Title.
BF724.3.E5C87   1986   152.4   85-43352
ISBN 0-684-18571-7

1 3 5 7 9 11 13 15 17 19 F / C 20 18 16 14 12 10 8 6 4 2

Printed in the United States of America

Contents

ONE

Darkness into Light

"There can be no transforming of darkness into light and of apathy into movement without emotion." Thus the great Swiss psychoanalyst Carl Jung characterized emotion, that quality of behavior that is the very essence of life. Without emotion, life itself is inanimate; it is impossible to be alive without experiencing emotion. When we talk with people who fail to react to what we are saying, when we watch a tennis match between two robotlike players, or when we read a novel that lacks feeling, we know what it is to experience the dull and lifeless.

Emotions are important not only for the preservation of health but for survival itself. Emotions permit us to communicate. Only when we understand our own feelings and the feelings of others can we have healthy interrelationships.

Although emotions are with us throughout life, there is heightened awareness of them during the adolescent years — a stage of life that is characterized by rapid mood swings, along with a great deal of anxiety and insecurity. A knowledge of emotions and of how they affect the body can help us see to it that they work for and not against us.

1

Webster defines **emotion*** as "a departure from the normal calm state of an organism, of such nature as to include strong feeling, an impulse toward open action, and certain internal physical reactions; any one of the states designated as fear, anger, love, hate, desire, disgust, grief, joy, surprise, etc." Emotions generally are pleasant or unpleasant, or to use a more psychological description, positive or negative.

The word *emotion* is derived from the Latin *emovere* — *e* meaning "out" and *movere* meaning "to move." Thus the word means to move out from or away from something — away from our usual relatively stable psychological and physical condition. Emotion is a dynamic experience that changes our baseline state.

Some investigators distinguish *emotion* from *feeling*, considering feeling to be only one part of an emotion — the inner, subjective sensation without including the physiological response. But in everyday usage, in literature, and in this book, the words are used synonymously.

Human beings have always been fascinated by feelings. In ancient times emotions were thought to reside in a specific part of the body. The Hindus and Chinese believed that the seat of emotions was located in the chest and abdomen, that emotions entered these areas via the mouth at birth and at the time of death escaped through the top of the skull.

Feelings abound in the language of the Bible. The first book of the Old Testament, Genesis, describing the birth of humanity, states that "God created light and saw that it was *good.*" So the first feeling in the Bible is positive. Later, when

---

*Words and phrases printed in boldface type are defined in the glossary beginning on page 121.

Adam and Eve were created and ignored the specific instructions to avoid eating the fruit of the apple tree, the Lord decreed that "I will put enmity between thee and the woman" and to Eve he said "in sorrow thou shalt bring forth children" and "thy desire shall be to thy husband." Later, Cain "was very wroth, and his countenance fell," Noah was told that "the fear of you and the dread of you shall be upon every beast of the earth," and when Abraham fell asleep, "an horror of great darkness fell upon him." Then in the New Testament, Joseph was told to "fear not to take unto thee Mary thy wife: for that which is conceived in her is of the Holy Ghost," John the Baptist asked: "O generation of vipers, who hath warned you to flee from the wrath to come?" and the Lord declared when speaking of Jesus: "This is my beloved Son in whom I am well pleased."

But despite all this chronicling of emotions, no systematic treatment of the subject appears in the Bible. It was a Greek, Empedocles, who stated that the universe was composed of four elements — fire, air, earth, and water. Hippocrates, known today as the father of medicine, adopted this idea of the elements and either he or his followers carried it a step further; they suggested that these four components of nonliving matter combined into qualities of warm-moist (fire and water), cold-dry (earth and air), warm-dry (fire and air), and cold-moist (earth and water). When these combined elements entered the body, they became the humors — blood, black bile, yellow bile, and phlegm. Probably these body fluids had been observed while treating battlefield injuries and illnesses. For a person to be healthy, thought the Greeks, these humors had to be in harmonious balance. Hippocrates, first to make the connection between the brain and emotions, said that overheating of the brain from too much bile caused terror and fear, as evidenced by a flushed face; overcooling of the brain from too much phlegm resulted in anxiety and grief.

Aristotle, one of the first people to observe attitudes and reactions scientifically, believed that emotion was limited to a pleasure feeling and a pain feeling. We perceive through the senses, which experiences bring pleasure or pain. Consequently we learn to desire the pleasurable and avoid the painful. Finally, we react by moving toward something pleasurable and away from something painful. Sensible enough! But Aristotle was convinced that the heart was the place where emotions resided and that the only function of the brain was to keep the heart cool. It didn't matter that Aristotle was wrong about that. His concept of heart has been with us ever since. How many popular love songs have been written about the brain?

About the same time, Epicurus was defining philosophy as the art of making life happy. He believed in pleasure in moderation and declared that a person is altruistic because it gives pleasure to make others happy.

Finally, Galen, a Greek physician who settled in Rome, originated the concept of the four temperaments, each derived from a preponderance of one of the humors. He labeled these "sanguine" from blood, "choleric" from yellow bile, "phlegmatic" from phlegm, and "melancholic" from black bile. Choleric people were quick to anger, phlegmatic people were apathetic and slow-moving, sanguine people were courageous, hopeful, and amorous, and melancholics were gloomy.

We still dub people melancholic, choleric, sanguine, and phlegmatic although we know that these temperaments are not caused by an overabundance of bile or blood or phlegm.

And we still say that people are in a good or bad "humor."

Very little progress in the study of emotions was made from the time of those ancient Greek physicians until this century although Francis Hutcheson, a renowned seventeenth-century philosopher from Dublin, wrote about the "passions" and classified them into five senses, and a century later Alexander Bain, professor of philosophy at the University of London, showed amazing foresight in linking physiology with emotions. His concepts would not be proved in the laboratory until 70 more years had passed. In 1884, William James proposed a fundamental inclusive theory of emotion.

TWO

The Range of Feelings

We humans possess an amazing spectrum of emotions. Not only that, we can express every individual emotion in a range that varies from barely noticeable to violent. Like an expert violinist, we can play hundreds of emotional "notes," and each one can be played in any amplitude from soft to loud. Emotions can combine to intensify an already pleasant or unpleasant feeling. Frequently, however, emotions are conflicting. We may want to get a certain job but if we lack confidence, a part of us may be hoping that we'll be turned down. Such contradictory feelings are termed ambivalent.

When an emotional state persists, it is called a mood. For example, if we feel happy over a period of time, we are said to be in a good mood.

We begin with two unpleasant emotions, **anger** and **fear.** Positive emotions like **love**, **joy**, curiosity, and **determination** are important in the way we adapt to life and live it, but anger and fear are vital to the survival of an individual in a life-threatening situation.

ANGER

One of the most easily recognized emotions, anger is "a strong feeling of displeasure and usually of antagonism."* We become angry when we've been injured in certain ways that seem unfair to us. (What is fair or unfair depends on the particular culture we live in; in each culture, we expect and anticipate appropriate behavior.) There are many synonyms for angry states, some of which are truly synonymous but others of which have slightly different meanings reflecting the degree of anger. Thus ire is stronger than simple anger, rage and fury stronger yet and suggesting some loss of self-control, and wrath as strong as fury but with an implication that revenge or punishment is sought for the wrong that has been done. Rage often occurs when something or someone has hampered or checked some action that we wish to pursue. It is a reaction to frustration. Obviously, as the meanings of these words differ somewhat from one another, so too do the emotional states that they describe.

FEAR

Fear is an "agitated foreboding often of some real or specific peril." Again, many synonyms for fear have a somewhat different meaning. Dread adds to fear the idea of reluctance to face the person or situation causing the fear. Fright is sudden, startling, and short-lived fear. Terror is extreme fear or dread that could lead to panic. Panic is overpowering and unreasoning fear, usually manifested by frantic activity. Horror is

---

*This and other quoted definitions of emotions are from *Webster's Third New International Dictionary*.

fear combined with strong repugnance or shuddering revulsion. Trepidation is a trembling fear caused by timidity.

There are many different types of fears. As children, we often fear our own feelings, irrationally believing that a hate-filled wish can result in actual harm toward someone. There are fears of death, fears of being hurt or injured, fears of being different from other people, fears of failure: the list goes on and on. Often, we do not fear what we think we fear. For example, the real meaning of one of the most common fears — fear of the dark — was accidentally uncovered by Sigmund Freud. These are his own words about that discovery:

> For the explanation of the origin of the infantile fear, I am indebted to a three-year-old boy whom I once heard calling from a dark room: 'Auntie, talk to me, I am afraid because it is dark.' 'How will that help you,' answered the aunt, 'you cannot see anyhow.' 'That's nothing,' answered the child, 'if someone talks, then it becomes light.' He was, as we see, not afraid of darkness, but he was afraid because he missed the person he loved, and he promised to calm down as soon as he was assured of her presence.

ANXIETY

Anxiety is "a state of . . . experiencing a strong or dominating blend of uncertainty, agitation or dread, and brooding fear about some contingency." In short, anxiety is the fear that something *may* happen that will hurt us. The uncertainty of this fear is its cardinal feature. Anxiety usually lasts longer than does simple fear, particularly in our fast-paced and often impersonal civilization. *Uneasiness* is a synonym. Although anxiety belongs to the fear family, it has been defined separately because the nagging quality of anxiety differs distinctly from the emotional states produced by the other forms of fear. An anxious person may know what he or she is anxious about, but often the cause of the anxiety is unknown. Pervasive uneasiness without conscious knowledge of what is causing it is called **free-floating anxiety**.

HATE

Hate is a sustained emotion in which strong dislike is combined with ill will toward the hated object. Because of that second factor — wanting something unpleasant to happen to the offending person or situation — hate is more powerful than simple dislike.

DISGUST

Disgust is a "physical or emotional reaction comparable to nausea that is excited by exposure to something highly distasteful or loathsome." Situations that disgust us figuratively or literally make us sick.

GUILT

Guilt comprises "feelings of culpability, especially for imagined offenses or from a sense of inadequacy: morbid self-reproach often manifest in marked preoccupation with the moral correctness of one's behavior." The word *imagined* in the above definition is used in its broadest sense and does not mean imaginary only; one can feel guilty over real offenses as well. Essentially, a person feels guilty because some action that person has taken doesn't live up to a moral or intellectual standard that he or she values. There is a lot of "should have" in guilt, implying that the person was capable of acting in a better manner. Without the development of a conscience during childhood, a person will be incapable of feeling guilt.

SORROW

Sorrow is "uneasiness or anguish due to loss (as of something loved or familiar)." There are many forms of sorrow. Grief is painfully sharp and extended sorrow. Anguish is excruciating, torturing grief. Regret means a sorrow that usually is not outwardly shown. It frequently represents spiritual or mental anguish caused by disappointment, lost opportunity, or heartache and may be either fleeting or long-lasting.

EMBARRASSMENT

Embarrassment is "a state of self-conscious distress" caused by certain situations or by the actions of a person or persons. Often, what causes embarrassment hampers the free choice of action of an individual so that while the discomfort is going on, he or she is "stuck" for the moment and is in the presence of others witnessing this discomfort. This presence of other people, or at least awareness that other people know what has happened to make a situation embarrassing, seems to be the most important feature of this emotion. When someone is embarrassed, other emotional overtones may be present. *Abashed* implies that the person had prior self-confidence, which was checked by the embarrassing incident. Frequently, an embarrassed person becomes rattled, which means that the embarrassment has resulted in so much agitation that mental processes have become disorganized. Humiliation adds to a feeling of embarrassment a loss of self-esteem caused by the derision of others.

ENVY

Envy is a "painful or resentful awareness of the advantage enjoyed by another, accompanied by a desire to possess the same advantage." Anything that seems desirable and is possessed by someone else can be envied — achievements, physical and mental attributes, freedom, jobs, money, etc., and what is most envied often reflects the values of the family and the community.

JEALOUSY

Jealousy, a very close relative of envy, is the state in which "one is intolerant of rivalry or unfaithfulness." Jealousy is an extremely painful emotion, particularly when love or affection is involved, because when the person we care for greatly chooses another over ourselves, we suffer a loss of self-esteem. In the case of romantic love, this involves one's perceptions about one's femininity or masculinity. Because of insecurity (or in the classic case of Othello, false information maliciously supplied), jealousy frequently is unjustified; frequently the loved person's feelings haven't changed, only the jealous person's perception of them.

Even emotions considered to be "pure" are themselves mixtures. Jealousy, for example, certainly includes elements of both anger and anxiety.

SURPRISE

Surprise is the state of being taken unawares without any time for preparation. It is the opposite of anticipation, which emotion prevents surprise. Astonishment is the state that exists when one is struck "with a sudden sense of surprise or wonder, especially through something unexpected or difficult to accept as true or reasonable." Astonishment has that quality of wonder that the more commonly experienced "surprise" usually lacks.

ANTICIPATION

Anticipation involves giving advance thought to something so that surprise is avoided. A person who anticipates knows what's coming or what to expect. Anticipation also commonly refers to looking forward with pleasure (or displeasure) to something that will occur at some future time.

LOVE

Love is "the attraction, desire, or affection felt for a person who arouses delight or admiration or elicits tenderness, sympathetic interest, or benevolence." Love is the most fulfilling emotion of all, and the above definition is but one of its many meanings. It may represent a romantic attachment, a warm family relationship, a strong feeling of friendship, a religious adoration, a feeling about the interests one is pursuing, etc. Love has been shown to be essential for survival. Repeatedly, babies in understaffed institutions who were fed adequately but deprived of cuddling, touching, kissing, and other forms of caring have died. Nurture means more than food; it must include love.

JOY

Joy is "the emotion excited by the acquisition or expectation of good." Depending on the degree of joy, the emotion is manifested by merriment, gaiety, or in the case of extreme joy, by jubilation. When joy is prolonged, it is called happiness. Bliss is perfect happiness.

DESIRE

Desire is a "conscious impulse toward an object or experience that promises enjoyment or satisfaction in its attainment." Many researchers believe that all human behavior is the result of desire or stated another way, the search for pleasure. Synonyms for desire include urge, yearning, and longing. Curiosity is the desire to know and is the beginning point for many creative processes. Hope is desire when a future situation is uncertain.

DETERMINATION

Determination is defined as "ability to persist against opposition or attempts to dissuade or discourage." This is one of the most important positive emotions because it implies that the person believes that she or he, as an individual, has effective power and therefore accepts the challenge to accomplish some aim.

The above definitions tell us only what these major emotions are, but we want to know where in our bodies they originate as well as how our bodies react to manifest them. The next chapter deals with these questions.

THREE

Feelings: How and Why

We turn red in the face with anger or embarrassment, we become pale from fright and may break out in a cold sweat, and when we are nervous before an examination, the pulse speeds up, we have an "empty" feeling in the chest, and we have to urinate frequently. Some emotions produce physical activity, such as jumping for joy or pacing with anxiety, while others, such as sorrow, often may find us sitting motionless without desire to move. All these body reactions to emotion are known as physiological effects and indicate what a powerful influence the mind has over the body.

Emotions have a purpose. It's easy to see, for instance, why a little fear of water or of heights is a valuable safety mechanism. **Physiology** is the science that discovers why and how the various systems of the body, along with their component organs and tissues, do what they do.

All body systems — circulatory, digestive, endocrine, nervous, respiratory, and urinary — are involved in both causing emotions and responding to them. Strong emotion usually involves most of the systems.

Theories of emotion attempt to explain as many facts as possible: How do emotions originate? What is their purpose?

14

What effects do they have on the body? Have they evolved from lower species? Are they universal? Are they inherited? No one theory has answered all of these questions. (Technically, when theories are confirmed, they no longer are theories but become organized bodies of facts; but since they were called theories long before they were unequivocally proved, some still are designated by that name, despite the dictionary definition.)

Fundamental Theories

During the nineteenth and twentieth centuries, several theories concerning both the origin of emotions and their functions were proposed. There is general agreement now about where emotions come from. Emotions originate in the brain. It is amazing that the first man to perform dissection for scientific purposes, while not writing specifically about emotions, correctly inferred that thought, an important component of emotion, emanated from the brain. He was a physician named Alcmaeon, he came from Crotone, Italy, and he lived in the fifth century B.C.

There also is agreement that emotions do have a primary function — to protect the individual and species and aid in their survival. It has been said that the only permanent thing in life is change, and appropriate emotions appropriately expressed permit us to adapt to a constantly changing environment. Thus, helping in the process of **adaptation**—adjustment to a new set of conditions—is the major function of emotions.

The first important theory of emotions was proposed in 1884 by Harvard physiologist, anatomist, and psychologist, William James; as the result of independent research, it was published once again a year later by a Danish professor, Carl Lange. Known as the James-Lange theory, it was the prevailing view for almost a half-century, although that portion of the theory dealing with the origin of emotions was incorrect. James spoke first of the more primary emotions, which he termed "coarser" emotions: grief, fear, rage, love. Here are his own words, and the italics are his as well:

> Our natural way of thinking about these coarser emotions is that the mental perception of some fact excites the mental affection called the emotion, and this latter state of mind gives rise to the bodily expression. My theory, on the contrary, is that *the bodily changes follow directly the perception of the exciting fact and that our feeling of the same changes as they occur is the emotion.* Common sense says, we lose our fortune, are sorry and weep; we meet a bear, are frightened and run; we are insulted by a rival, are angry and strike.

James goes on to say that these commonsense conclusions are wrong because physiological body changes come before emotions. Therefore, he believed that we feel sorry because we cry, angry because we strike, afraid because we tremble, and not the reverse. What James is saying here, then, is that emotions do not emanate primarily from the brain. He believed that either the visceral organs (large internal organs such as stomach, heart, etc.) first perceived an "inner excitation" or that the brain perceived an idea but that this brief perception was the brain's only role in emotion. James thought that the response of the organic receptors, especially those receptors located in the viscera, was responsible for feelings.

The James-Lange theory was put to rest in 1927 by the work of another Harvard physiologist, Walter B. Cannon, who pointed out that experimental work had clearly shown that visceral perception is much slower than brain perception and could not possibly be the initiating factor of an emotion. He also performed experiments with cats, severing all nerve connections between the brain and organs like the heart, lungs, stomach, and bowels — all the visceral organs in which James believed feelings resided. He found that the emotional responses of the animals were unchanged. Cannon showed that the brain perception was the first step in the chain of emotional response. He suggested that the seat of emotions lay in a specialized, primitive part of the brain called the thalamus and suggested "circuits" to and from the thalamus. Thus, the brain, seemingly forgotten since the days of Alcmaeon and Hippocrates, assumed its rightful place in the origin of emotions.

Regarding the purpose of emotions, Cannon proposed a theory to explain the most fundamental and primitive function of emotions: their value in preparing animals and man for emergency action in situations of danger. Although his idea of a "center" of emotions located in the thalamus was too limited, Cannon's suggestion that brain circuits to and from the thalamus played an important role in emotions was a critical one.

This concept was embodied in a much more detailed theory proposed in 1937 by James W. Papez, professor of anatomy at Cornell University. Papez suggested that many parts of the brain and the interconnections between these parts "may elaborate the functions of central emotion, as well as participate in emotional expression." This concept of the complex connections among various critical brain structures became the cornerstone of our understanding of the brain's relationship to emotion.

Newer Concepts

Jean Piaget, a Swiss psychologist, devoted his long lifetime to the study of the intellectual and emotional development of children. He documented the increasingly varied and complex thoughts and feelings that developed as infants matured into children and children matured into adolescents.

Piaget outlined various stages of development. At the earliest stage, age 0 to 2, the infant learns to maintain an image of objects. A personal experiment helped Piaget to confirm this. When his daughter, Jacqueline, was 8 months old, he held a cigarette lighter in front of her and then dropped it. Jacqueline did not follow the path the lighter took but instead continued to look at her father's hand. Later, when Jacqueline was 19 months old, Piaget held a coin in his hand and then placed his hand under a blanket and hid the coin there. Now, she first looked at his hand and, finding it empty, immediately looked under the blanket and found the coin. Her brain had reached a stage mature enough to remember objects; further, she had learned an elementary form of reasoning; the coin was in the hand, the hand went under the blanket, the coin was not in the hand so the coin must be under the blanket.

During Piaget's second stage (age 2 to 7), the child begins to acquire language, begins dreaming and having night terrors, and is able to match words and symbols to the objects they represent.

During the next stage (age 7 to 11), the child can perform what Piaget calls "concrete operations." That means he can think about things and solve problems "in his head" but only in relation to his current situation. He cannot as yet draw generalizations from his knowledge that allow him to look ahead.

Piaget calls his last stage (age 12 to 15) "**formal operations**." During this period, adolescents have developed sufficient maturity to reflect about their thoughts, to form ideals and, because of advanced reasoning ability, to plan realistically for the future. From this time on, mental and emotional growth continues by the use of faculties already acquired, along with new experiences, to gain deeper understanding.

As body and brain mature, so too do emotions become more complex and varied. The only fears a tiny infant knows are a sudden startling noise, a pinprick, or a movement, when being held, that feels like loss of support. At birth, the baby is unaware of any world outside of himself and when his needs for food and comfort are not met, he responds by screaming his simple and pure anger. Emotions are the infant's only language.

Pleasure is first shown at about one to two months of age when the baby begins to respond to familiar faces by smiling. Still later, at about five to eight months, an infant shows more awareness of the outside world by exhibiting fear when strangers enter the room. Before that age, the baby usually is indifferent to the presence of strangers.

At later ages, around two years, five years, and early teens, the well-known periods of negativity come into play. Each of these stages represents emotional growth, even though parents might not think so. One father, lending his car to his independent adolescent son, said, "Have a good time." The boy answered, "Don't tell me what to do."

The classic studies of Piaget, along with those of Erik Erikson, Maria Montessori, and other investigators, have defined the relationship between behavior and emotions. Many new theories have been advanced about the origins, functions, components, and social role of emotions. All agree on the most important thing about emotions: the brain is paramount and always involved in the origin and complexity of emotions.

FOUR

The Nervous System

The nervous system, along with the **endocrine system**, provides most of the controlling functions for the body and therefore is of great importance in the physiology of emotion. It comprises the brain, spinal cord, and all the nerves of the body and their connections. This system receives and sends out the messages that control all the varied activities of our bodies. In general, the nervous system controls rapid activities such as the contraction of muscles, changes occurring in the visceral organs, and even the rate at which some endocrine glands secrete their hormones.

(The autonomic nervous system, as we shall see, controls the involuntary activity of visceral organs such as the heart, stomach, and intestines.) The central nervous system controls mental activity and *voluntary* physical activity.

The central nervous system consists of the brain and the spinal cord. The brain is a highly complex computer center, organizing and correlating the millions of messages continually received and transmitted during the lifetime of an individual. The spinal cord is a tube of nerve tissue traveling through the spinal column, a series of vertically stacked bones (vertebrae). The spinal cord connects all the nerves of the body to the

PROPERTY OF
ARAB PUBLIC LIBRARY
39888

brain. It contains incoming pathways to receive messages and outgoing pathways to send out impulses to muscles and glands. The central nervous system has two major functions — the control of all mental activity and the control of *voluntary* physical activity. For example, if your brain receives a message that you want to read a book that you spot lying on a nearby coffee table, the brain relays this message to the spinal cord, whence it continues out along the nerves that activate arm and finger muscles, allowing you to pick up the book.

The brain is divided into two parts: the upper cerebral cortex is the outgrowth of a more primitive second part, the lower brain, to which the cerebral cortex has many connections.

The Cerebral Cortex

The cerebral cortex is a huge sensory storehouse containing fifty billion nerve cells. Past experiences are stored here, as well as in a more primitive part of the brain called the limbic system. These stored experiences are called **memory**. Besides its memory function, the limbic system is the part of the brain from which emotions originate. Over three-quarters of all nerve cell bodies (neurons) are housed in the cerebral cortex.

The cerebral cortex is the control center for voluntary muscle activity. Each part of the body is controlled by a separate, specific area of the cerebral cortex; the distribution of these areas is very interesting because the size of the area in the cortex has nothing to do with the size of the body part it represents. The more precise and delicate the movement is, the larger the area that controls it. Thus, the trunk is represented by a very small area of cortex, whereas the thumb

FRONTAL SECTION OF THE CEREBRUM

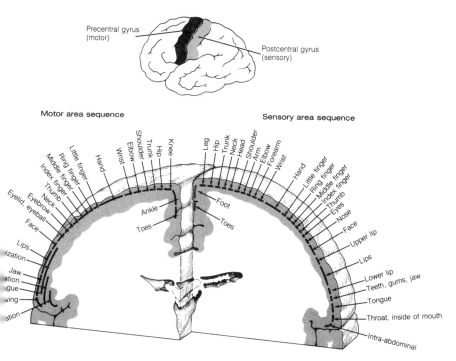

and fingers and lips, tongue, and vocal cords are controlled by a large area. Messages sent along the **motor pathways** on one side of the cerebral cortex control movements on the other side of the body. For example, the right arm and leg are controlled by the left side of the brain, and vice versa. But the performance of skilled acts is not limited to the hemisphere that originally controlled these highly discrete muscular movements. The Hungarian world-champion pistol shooter, K. Takacs, shot with his right arm until it was amputated in 1938 because of an accident. Subsequently, using his left arm, he won the world's championship in 1939 and Olympic gold medals in 1948 and 1952.

Scientists have shown that the two hemispheres of the brain, while having identical appearances, have different functions. The left half controls verbal functions, such as speaking, reading, and writing. The right half is responsible for visualizing the form of things, such as shapes of objects. It also seems to be the "feeling" half and therefore is responsible for much of our appreciation of music and art.

The memory of complicated motor movements, such as typing, is bound together in patterns called engrams. These engrams are formed after movements are repeated and repeated. When needed, the entire engram is then "pulled" from the memory bank and the complex motor movement performed. The arm and finger muscle movements required to pick up that book from the coffee table are stored in an engram and recalled when needed; thinking about how to perform the movement is not required.

An individual neuron operates on an "all or none" basis. The electrical impulse it carries is discharged either completely or not at all. Therefore, the only way of securing a graded muscle response is through variation of the *number* of neurons involved in the action. The more neurons discharging, the stronger the muscular response.

Sensory information is much more important for the performance of complicated movements than is the motor information. If a monkey has learned to perform a complex task and then parts of the motor cortex usually required are removed, the monkey is able to use other muscle groups to perform the task; however, if small areas of sensory cortex are removed, even though the motor cortex is intact, the monkey will not be able to perform that familiar task.

The Lower Brain

This part of the brain is subdivided into areas known as the medulla, pons, mesencephalon, hypothalamus, thalamus, cerebellum, and basal ganglia. What is important about this lower brain is, first, that it controls the more primitive emotions (stimulation of the thalamus and hypothalamus produces rage in monkeys) and, secondly, that it controls subconscious activities. In this role it is connected to the autonomic nervous system, which is located closer to the outside of the body than is the spinal cord. The subconscious control of arterial blood pressure and respiration, for instance, is centered largely in the medulla and in the pons.

We know that the lower brain by itself can produce emotional patterns of anger, sexual activities, and the like because these reactions occur in animals whose cerebral cortex has been removed. Intelligent control of emotions, however, depends on a balance between the "thinking" cortex and signals sent from the lower brain. It is the higher cortical centers that usually keep rage and other strong emotions under control. When the cortex is overwhelmed by a massive autonomic response causing many emotional messages to reach the cortex at the same time, the result is panic.

In concert with the lower brain, the autonomic nervous system controls those parts of the body — mainly organs and glands — that work automatically or without conscious effort. There is no need to "tell" the heart to beat or the stomach to

BRAIN

cerebrum
(showing left cerebral hemisphere)

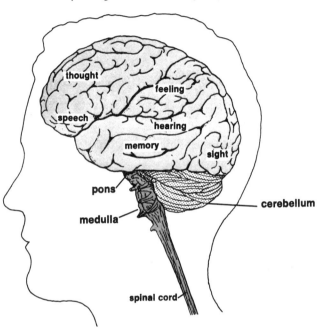

digest food; these organs perform those tasks automatically. But when emotion comes into play, their linkage to the brain is obvious. For example, with anger the stomach usually will churn and the heart beat faster.

Reflexes

Reflexes are an important part of autonomic activity as well as of voluntary muscle function. A reflex consists of automatic action that does not involve awareness by the brain. Everyone is familiar with the knee-jerk reflex that occurs when a physician taps the tendon below the kneecap and the leg jerks involuntarily, but there are thousands of other reflex actions.

For example, if you surprised someone by placing an ice cube against that person's arm, you would see a sudden withdrawal of the arm. This muscular response is the motor, or moving, part of a reflex arc; the nerves stimulating the muscles to contract have been previously stimulated by sensory nerves. The brain is not involved. When cold impulses travel to the spinal cord, the motor nerves in the spinal cord are stimulated and carry the message to move back to the arm. But there may be a strong emotional response immediately afterward, when the brain is put to work. The victim of that ice-cube experiment may become angry or may think it's funny and laugh or may simply be surprised that you would play a dirty trick like that. His or her reaction will depend on personality and also on how that person happens to be feeling at the time of your experiment.

One of the most important types of reflex is the *conditioned reflex*, first discovered and described by the great Russian physiologist, Ivan Pavlov. Pavlov demonstrated that a reflex, such as a dog's salivating at the sight of food, could be modified by conditioning the reflex to a different stimulus. By ringing a bell at the same time as food was presented, Pavlov taught the dog to associate the ringing of the bell and food. Eventually, the sound of the bell alone was sufficient to make the dog salivate. Memory thus plays a significant role in the conditioned reflex.

Conditioned behavior is very important in emotions. Stimuli that were pleasant or unpleasant in old situations can evoke the same feelings, even though the new situation is entirely

different. For instance, fright is a primitive emotion, valuable
for survival, and seems to alert us more than pleasurable
emotions do; if we've been conditioned to fear a series of
unfriendly dogs, the sight of any new dog may frighten us,
even though he's a friendly animal who wants to play rather
than attack. We can also be conditioned to associations with
unpleasantness. If we were attacked by a dog whose owner
wore a bright-green suit, at a later time just the sight of a
bright-green suit might cause uneasy feelings.

Wakefulness, Sleep, and Arousal

All activity, including emotional response, is different when
we are awake from when we are asleep. These two states are
controlled by that part of the lower brain called the mesencephalon (midbrain). There are nerve pathways between the
mesencephalon and the cerebral cortex, via the thalamus as
well as direct. When we are sufficiently rested, activity begins
in the mesencephalon and wakefulness ensues. With fatigue,
the mesencephalon, along with the thalamus and cerebral
cortex, becomes inactive and when this happens, we sleep.
Emotions have strong influence on sleep patterns; during the
dreaming portions of sleep — when emotions are in command
— we have rapid eye movements (REM), which can be easily
seen by an observer. Exciting or disturbing situations may
prevent sleep even in the presence of great fatigue, and by
the same token a well-rested person may yawn and become
sleepy when faced with a troublesome situation he or she
wants to avoid.

There is another kind of wakefulness, which psychologists
call arousal, and this type of awareness refers exclusively to

emotion. Arousal is a nonspecific internal stimulation that alerts the organism and permits emotional and behavioral activity.

Thinking, Feeling, and Past Experience

It is obvious that past experience plays an important part of thinking and feeling. Knowing in advance what damage a speeding car can do makes us react differently from the way we would if we never had seen or heard a large object collide with a small object.

Thinking and feeling interact and are almost never independent of each other. If we think about almost anything with which we've had previous experience, there will be an emotional response to the subject or situation that is occupying our thoughts; often, these thoughts are not at the conscious level — they're unconscious — but nevertheless, they're there and we react emotionally.

There are times when physical changes in the body, such as the release of **hormones** or the action of medications or other chemical substances, cause emotional responses. All emotional responses, however, even those caused by chemical changes, involve brain activity.

The Senses and Memory

We receive all the information we have about the outside world from our **senses**. They are the outposts of the nervous system, and the information they transmit to the brain is being constantly stored in its cerebral cortex and in its limbic system. Our emotional reaction to any situation is formed largely from all of this information we've been storing up since birth, which we call memory.

The senses are specialized mechanisms comprising connected nerve cells, which allow us to receive and respond to both external and internal stimuli. The connections between nerve cells are called **synapses**; as a result of nerve stimulation, impulses travel along the nerve and when they reach the synapse, the neurons secrete excitatory substances that permit transmission of the impulse across the synapse and along the adjoining cell. Other substances are secreted that inhibit or prevent the passage of nerve impulses.

Sight, hearing, smell, taste, and cutaneous (skin) sensation are the external senses that relay information from the outside world to the spinal cord and brain. The brain discards as unimportant about 99 percent of the sensory information it receives; for example, we rarely are aware of the pressure exerted on the skin by the clothes we wear but if it rains, the discomfort of wet clothes reminds us to change into dry garments.

In addition to these five external senses, we possess extremely important internal senses: the kinesthetic (perception of movement) senses and the organic senses located in internal organs of the digestive and respiratory systems and in the walls of blood vessels. The physical sensations accompanying the emotions — fear, for example, with its "butterflies in the stomach," "empty" feeling in the chest, heart pounding, etc. — originate from these organic senses whose **receptors** are located deep inside the body.

Information relayed by the sensory pathways begins with the receptors. Receptors are tiny cells located in the various sense organs, and they are the first parts of the body to receive sensory messages, such as light, sound, heat, and cold, from the outside world. These receptors are located inside organs and tissues, parts of the body that perform a specialized job. The organs of sight are the eyes, the organs of hearing are the ears, the organ of smell is the nose, the organs of taste are both the nose and the tongue. All of these organs are small. The skin is the largest organ, and cutaneous sensation comes from receptors spread all over the surface of the body.

Various cutaneous sensations include light touch, hot, cold, and pain. Some cutaneous sensations like itching and tickling seem to be combinations of pain and touch. Pain has no specialized receptors; the naked nerve endings of the nerve fibers transmitting the sensation of pain serve that purpose. Another sensation, pressure, is closely allied to the skin sensations but its receptors, the Pacinian corpuscles, actually lie beneath the skin and their nerve fibers travel mostly in the sensory nerves supplying tendons and blood vessels. (Newer evidence raises the possibility that all of these receptors can respond to a variety of stimuli so that the sensation of pain, for example, could be transmitted along touch pathways.)

One of the internal senses is **proprioception**, the position sense. Its receptors in the nervous system, proprioceptors, relay information about the exact position of the various parts of the body at any one time. For example, we know without looking where our feet are when we walk or we would constantly be tripping and falling. The proprioceptors are located throughout muscles and tendons and are present in the labyrinth, that part of the inner ear that regulates balance.

The most important thing to remember about sense organs

and their receptors is that, with the exception of reflex activity, all the information they provide goes to the brain, where the information is integrated with messages from other parts of the brain and sent back to the periphery for action. Essentially, we see, hear, smell, taste, etc., with our brain. In fact, it is possible for a blind person to receive visual information by use of wires implanted directly into the visual cortex of the brain.

We can see the importance of the senses in relaying information that will result in emotional responses. Consider once again that speeding car, whizzing around the corner. We see it with our eyes, even if it's only a blur. Probably our peripheral vision transmits the information that something is racing toward us. We hear the sound of the car coming and possibly the sounds of the brakes screeching, if the driver happens to see us. We may smell the exhaust fumes, and our skin will feel the rush of air as the car races by. Then our muscular responses and balance come into play as we jump backward to avoid getting hit. We've called on a lot of senses so far during this adventure.

One further sense comes into play: The incident leaves us with a figurative bad taste in our mouth. Past knowledge of the implications of such a close shave causes us to have other, more complex emotions. We know from past experience (not only from our personal experience but from hearing and reading about other people in similar situations) that reckless driving can injure and kill. As we think about that while we stand shaken on the sidewalk, we are not only angry and resentful but also relieved that we weren't hit. Feeling this way, we are experiencing several emotions simultaneously, some of them conflicting.

Instincts

The inherited patterns of behavior called **instincts** are the exception to the rule that behavior patterns depend on memory-storing and other sensory input and output. These complex instinctual survival patterns don't rely on current information supplied by the senses but rather are passed from one generation to the next in genetic material, the DNA. For example, a mother cat giving birth to her first litter of kittens has neither seen nor experienced this process before. Yet, she instinctively knows exactly how to proceed after the kittens are born and she frees them from the birth membranes, bites the umbilical cords to separate them from the placentas, licks them clean — without which cleaning the kittens will not urinate and will die from kidney failure — carries them correctly, and then positions herself to nurse the new arrivals.

The sum total of all this brain activity we have discussed in this chapter results in what is called the *mind*. While it comprises the total conscious and unconscious content of thoughts and feelings, usually when we talk about the mind we are referring to the brain's memory and thinking functions.

FIVE

The Endocrine System

The endocrine system consists of a small group of specialized glands that secrete powerful chemicals called hormones directly into the circulating blood. A gland is a group of cells that manufactures and secretes substances for body use. The hormones endocrine glands make and secrete cause emotional changes, some of them profound. We know that the nervous system has significant control over emotions and that the control can be exercised in two ways: by the direct action of the autonomic nervous system and by stimulating the hormone output of the endocrine glands. Usually, both actions are at work.

THE PITUITARY GLAND

The **pituitary** gland, located in the brain, is known as the master gland because many of the hormones it secretes act on the other endocrine glands. Newer research has discovered many brain hormones in addition to those secreted by the pituitary; they originate in the hypothalamus and other portions of the brain. Other endocrine glands are:

ENDOCRINE SYSTEM

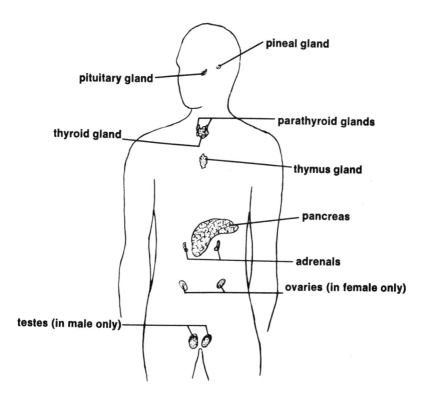

THE ADRENAL GLANDS

The paired **adrenal glands** are located above the kidneys and control the salt-and-water balance of the body. If they failed to function, we could not survive without receiving adrenal hormones manufactured by pharmaceutical companies. The adrenals, in addition to their salt-and-water function, also produce hormones that reduce inflammation (cortisone is the best known of these) and hormones that are important for sexual development. Cortisone administered in high doses over a long period of time often causes the emotional change known as euphoria. In this state, the person experiences a sense of well-being. All is happiness—but this type of euphoria is caused by a chemical change rather than by good things happening to that person.

The middle portion of the adrenal, its medulla, manufactures adrenaline, which is secreted when stressful situations arise, especially when great fear or anger is present. Adrenaline prepares the body for emergencies primarily by speeding the heart rate, raising the blood pressure, and acting on the liver to release glucose for energy.

THE THYROID GLAND

This single gland is located in the neck and controls metabolism, the rate at which the body uses food. The **thyroid**, along with the pituitary, plays an important role in growth. When the gland is overactive in the condition called hyperthyroidism, several emotional effects usually appear. Nervousness is prominent, along with irritability, restlessness, and a change in personality. Also, because of a shortened attention span, school problems often develop. With hypothyroidism, when the gland is underactive, lethargy is the most prominent behavioral change.

THE PARATHYROID GLANDS

These four tiny glands, located inside or behind the thyroid, control the calcium balance of the body. With **parathyroid** disorders, there may be some emotional changes but they are not a prominent part of the picture.

PANCREAS

The **pancreas** makes the hormone insulin, which controls the use of sugars by the body. The pancreas also secretes digestive **enzymes** through a duct into the bowel (an exocrine function, as opposed to the endocrine release of insulin directly into the bloodstream).

REPRODUCTIVE GLANDS

The **ovaries** and **testes** are the endocrine glands that affect sexual activity and reproduction and will be discussed in the section on puberty that follows.

Puberty and Adolescence

Puberty, a period of rapid biological growth, marks the beginning of **adolescence**, which continues for several years after puberty itself is over. Social and intellectual growth mark the later stages of adolescence.

In females, the onset of puberty may take place anywhere from age 8 to 14, with the average onset at age 12. Heredity is probably the most important factor in determining the age at which puberty starts. Puberty in females lasts about 3½ years. Males begin puberty somewhat later than do females, but again, there is much variation in the age at which puberty begins. Not only does male puberty start later than it does in females, but it lasts approximately a year longer.

One of the most important features of puberty is that when it is completed, there is ability to reproduce sexually. It is the time when males are capable of producing sperm and becoming fathers, and females, because their ovaries begin releasing ova (eggs) are physically able to conceive. Two major types of changes occur during puberty:

1. There is rapid development of the primary sex organs, which leads to their maturation. In the female, these organs are the uterus, vagina, and breasts; in the male, primary sex organs are the penis, testes, and prostate. During puberty, boys become capable of ejaculating seminal fluid containing active spermatazoa, whereas the sexual maturity of girls arrives when the menstrual cycle begins. This starting up of menstrual periods is called the **menarche**; it occurs around two and a half years after the beginning of puberty.

2. The secondary sex characteristics, which include growth of pubic, axillary (underarm), and facial hair, appear in both males and females, and they are accompanied by a growth spurt that primarily is the result of the lengthening of the long bones of the legs. Late in puberty, there is an increase in muscle strength.

The growth spurt of puberty and adolescence is the result of growth hormone secreted from the pituitary gland as well as from the growth effects of the sex hormones; it often continues in males until age 20, whereas the full stature of females has usually been reached by ages 17 to 19. Female bone growth involves widening of the pelvis; in the male, growth of the larynx precedes the change of voice that takes place.

These changes all result from endocrine secretion. The pituitary gland, since the age of six, has steadily increased its stimulation of the ovaries of females and the testes of males to produce the sex hormones estrogen and testosterone. But a sudden increase in pituitary stimulation of these organs signals the start of puberty. Sexual feelings, which have been present since birth, now markedly increase because of the hormonal changes resulting in sexual development.

The physical changes described above are accompanied by profound emotional changes. Erik Erikson, a pioneer child psychoanalyst, declared:

> To grow means to be divided into different parts which move at different rates. A growing boy has trouble in mastering his gangling body as well as his divided mind. He wants to be good, if only out of expediency, and always finds that he has been bad. He wants to rebel, and finds that almost against his will, he has given in. As his time perspective permits a glimpse of approaching adulthood, he finds himself acting like a child.

This period is characterized by understandable confusion. So many things are happening so fast that it's hard to get them into perspective. Adolescents should understand that they are not alone and that their peers are experiencing similar anxieties about physical appearance, sexual development, dating, popularity, and all the other problems that cause so much worry to teen-agers.

Adolescence is the period when "formal operations" thinking emerges and becomes fully developed. There is wide variation in the appearance and maturation of formal thinking, but on the average, it begins at age 12 and is complete by age 16. With the onset of puberty, the adolescent is absorbed by the rapid changes taking place in his or her body, whereas later, when the greatest growth spurt has been completed, a more stable body image is formed. Now the adolescent can concentrate on his or her thinking, can form abstract thoughts and can generalize. These capabilities, provided by "formal" thinking, allow planning for the future.

During this period, the adolescent establishes an identity separate from that of the family and at the same time achieves intellectual, sexual, and functional individuality. In short, he or she begins to understand and assert that wonderful (but frightening at first) feeling of "self." Eventually, a more equal relationship develops between adolescent and parents.

Certain problems unique to adolescence cause emotional turmoil. Because of the increased endocrine stimulation and resultant growth spurt, concerns about the body are always present. Besides specific concerns about the changes that are occurring in sexual organs, there is a heightened awareness of every part of the body. All sorts of physical worries emerge. Does this new mole that just appeared mean that something is seriously wrong with me? Does this pain in the chest mean I have heart disease? At one time or another during adolescence, many of the natural aches and pains and body changes associated with growth seem frightening.

At the same time that physical symptoms are worrisome, social relationships also are causing emotional stress. Why are my parents being stubborn about the time I get home at night? Why did every other girl except me get an invitation to the prom? Why am I so "unpopular"? Is it important to *be* "popular"? Do you have to have a lot of friends or is it O.K. to have one or two good friends? Why don't girls like me the way they do the other guys?

The questions go on and on because adolescence is when much preparation for adult life is taking place and for the first time, the ability to form a system of values based on individual ideas of what constitutes morality—what really is "right or wrong"—is present and being used. Thinking about and analyzing daily experiences and situations enable adolescents to form decisions about how they really feel about things. While doing so, they develop personal codes of morality.

SIX

Cannon's Experiments

Physiologist Walter B. Cannon proposed the famous **fight-or-flight** theory. When strong emotions are perceived by the brain, the autonomic nervous system begins to act. This division of the nervous system, in addition to its own primary actions, stimulates the adrenal gland to secrete adrenaline (also called adrenalin or epinephrine). The combined actions of the nervous system and various hormones like adrenaline prepare animals and humans for emergency action in dangerous situations. More recent observations have shown that there are many behavioral variations to the fight-or-flight situation; a signal of submission, for example, may represent flight without the animal or human actually running away from the perceived danger.

Cannon continuously studied the physiology of emotion in his laboratories at Harvard, and he and his associates compiled a significant body of important research. Surface signs of excitement — the pouring out of "cold sweat," the stopping of saliva flow so that the "tongue cleaves to the roof of the mouth," the rapid beating of the heart — had been clear to see. But what about the organs hidden deep in the body? Cannon wondered. His experiments would explain how the nervous system and adrenals act on these organs when emotions are involved.

Pavlov had already shown that the flow of gastric juice in the stomach of a dog was associated not with the presence of food itself but with the dog's appetite and his liking for the food. Cannon then performed experiments that showed that when a hungry dog was exposed to a cat that made him furious, he would eat, but the gastric secretion that had been present previously almost disappeared. Moreover, the dog's blood was found to have in it a high amount of adrenaline, which inhibits gastric juice secretions and stomach contractions.

Just as gastric juice secretion is related to emotions, so too is the secretion of saliva. In India, the dry mouth that occurs with anxiety was used for the "ordeal of rice." In this type of trial, several persons accused of a crime were all given rice to chew and then to spit it out on the leaves of the sacred fig tree; if the ejected rice showed little saliva in the chewer's mouth, that person was considered to be filled with fear and therefore guilty.

The adrenaline secreted under conditions of pain or emotional stress produces many other physiological effects. It causes liberation of sugar from the liver into the bloodstream; it relaxes the smooth muscles of the bronchioles, the smallest "breathing tubes" in the lungs; it causes more rapid blood clotting; in conjunction with nerve stimulation, it causes the spleen to contract and squeeze blood out, thus providing an extra supply of red blood cells (a self-transfusion); it alters the distribution of the blood in the body, driving it out of the abdominal organs so that more blood will be available in those organs needed for emergency functioning — the heart, lungs, central nervous system, and limbs — and raises the blood pressure. These organs depend on a general increase of blood pressure during emergencies because there are no nerves in the brain or lungs that cause blood vessels to decrease in diameter and there are more blood vessels open in the heart and muscles during times of increased activity; increased pressure is needed to ensure that sufficient blood gets to those parts. The faster flow with increased blood pressure allows more oxygen to be breathed in and exchanged for the carbon dioxide that must be eliminated by the lungs.

Cannon's experiments showing that strong emotion increased the amount of sugar in the blood, some of which appeared in the urine, began in 1911 and led to the conclusion that the sugar released provided the chief source of energy for the great muscular exertion needed during an emergency. Both fear and anger are likely to be followed by actions that require massive muscular exertion. Anger often leads to fighting, which in turn results in muscular activity and pain. Darwin wrote that "great pain urges all animals, and has urged them during countless generations, to make the most violent and diversified efforts to escape from the cause of suffering."

Cannon also performed an important series of experiments showing that fatigue causes a secretion of adrenaline, which in addition to its other effects raises the blood pressure. This rise in blood pressure, combined with the energy supplied when adrenaline acts on the liver to release sugar (glucose), is probably responsible for the phenomenon of "second wind," which all athletes, particularly runners, have experienced. Exhaustion is followed by a new surge of energy thanks to the actions of adrenaline.

Many strong emotions, particularly fear, stimulate the secretion of adrenaline. Amazing feats of strength are demonstrated under these conditions. Cannon tells the true story of John Colter, who, along with a companion, was seized in Montana by Indians and stripped naked. His companion resisted and was hacked to death but the chief made signs to Colter to head across the prairie. When Colter looked back, he saw the younger warriors grabbing their spears, and he knew that he was not being released but rather was to be chased and caught and scalped. He started to run even before he heard the war whoops. "Fear and hope lent a supernatural vigor to his limbs, and the rapidity of his flight astonished himself." After three miles, his strength began to wane, but only one pursuer was still after him. The Indian tried to kill Colter but fell, and Colter grabbed the spear, killed the Indian, and began to run again, his strength renewed; he told a friend later that after the struggle, he felt that he hadn't even run a mile. The frenzied excitement of certain religious ceremonies (Holy Rollers, dervishes) and of athletic rivalries where spectators and players alike are "pumped up" produce similar, if less dramatic, displays of energy.

What then is the significance of the increased energy and all of the other effects caused by fear and pain and rage? What are the emergency functions of the sympathico-adrenal system (the sympathetic division of the autonomic nervous system in association with the adrenaline, a hormone with sympathetic-like actions)? With these questions, Cannon asked himself how to interpret his research. Many of the answers were already evident.

The most significant feature of the bodily actions he had observed in pain and emotion-producing situations was that the reactions were in the nature of reflexes, "beyond the control of the will" and that their function was to protect.

Food, water and oxygen are required for existence. Survival depends not on memory or volition, but on insistent sensations and desires (such as thirst) that reflexly control these essential functions of eating, drinking, and breathing. Thus, sucking, swallowing, vomiting, and coughing are reflexes favoring the continuation of existence. And the sum total of the reflex effects of sympathetic nerve stimulation plus the additive action of adrenaline is to promptly prepare the organism for combat in the presence of the emotion rage or for flight in the event of great fear. Thus, these primitive emotions, rage and fear, aid in survival; this function is the basis for the fight-or-flight theory.

Tom's Stomach

In the 1940's there was a rare opportunity to get a direct look at physiological reactions to emotional situations. A 56-year-old maintenance man at New York Hospital, known in the scientific work as "Tom," agreed to be studied in the laboratory of Drs. Harold G. Wolff and Stewart Wolf. Both of these physicians had a special interest in the study of emotions.

Tom had a unique personal history. When he was nine years old, his father had bought some clam chowder in a saloon and brought it home in a beer pail. Tom came in from playing, thought the can contained cold beer, and drank some. The soup was extremely hot. Afraid that his mother would be angry if he spat it out, Tom swallowed it and immediately felt a burning sensation in his mouth, throat, and abdomen. Then he lost consciousness. He was taken to a hospital where a gastrotomy (an operation that leaves a hole in the stomach) was performed because his esophagus had been so badly burned that it became scarred and too narrow to permit the passage of food. From that time on, his mother fed him liquids through a tube to his stomach, but after she died, Tom chewed his food and then put it into the hole in his stomach so it could be digested.

The laboratory study of Tom took place in the morning, and he did his maintenance work in the afternoon. Each morning he arrived with an empty stomach. His stomach would be looked at through the opening in his abdominal wall, stomach contractions would be measured by a balloon connected to a recording device, the amount and acidity of his stomach secretions would be measured, and notes would be made by the researchers concerning Tom's mood, thoughts, and preoccupation during the experiments.

An attempt was made to classify his dominant emotion as (1) pleasurable excitement, (2) affection, (3) doubt, (4) fear, (5) frustration, (6) tension, (7) guilt, (8) sadness, (9) anxiety, (10) hostility, (11) resentment, or (12) disgust.

During the first experiments performed, it was observed that when food was discussed, Tom's stomach would get redder than normal and the amount of hydrochloric acid secreted would increase. When food was presented to him, the redness and acid increased. Surprisingly, when he actually got to taste the food, not much more reaction occurred. Following the study on food and for the rest of the time Tom worked in the lab, the effects on his stomach caused by various emotional states were studied and recorded. Here are some of the situations that presented themselves and Tom's reactions to them:

FEAR

An angry doctor came into the lab one morning looking for an experimental protocol that Tom had misplaced the previous afternoon. Fearful of the doctor's discovering that he was to blame for the disappearance of the document, Tom stayed silent and motionless, and his face became pale. He thought that he might lose the job he needed to support his family. At this point, his stomach was studied and it was noted that its lining became pale — it blanched from 90 to 20 degrees of redness — and remained pale until the doctor located the missing protocol and left the laboratory. During this period, acid secretion was greatly decreased.

DEPRESSIVE THOUGHTS

One day, Tom lost the lease on his home. He had been promised that he would have an opportunity to renew, but he failed to be present when the new lease was supposed to be signed and somebody else got his apartment. He became sad and resigned and exhibited absolutely no desire to fight back and change the unfair situation. Added to his sadness were feelings of self-reproach. When his stomach was studied, its reactions were similar to those shown when he was frightened. There was prolonged pallor, and secretion was markedly decreased. Taking beef broth, which usually increased the redness of his stomach, this time had practically no effect and the stomach remained pale. Tom had no appetite during this period, and in fact felt nauseated; in addition to the pallor, his stomach motility (movement) decreased, as evidenced by reduced contractions of his stomach muscles.

RESENTMENT AND HOSTILITY

One afternoon, Tom was particularly busy taking various laboratory tests for the doctors' studies. The tests were time-consuming and Tom thought he should get some kind of special consideration for the extra work involved, but nobody seemed to care about that. The following morning when he talked to the doctors about his anger, his stomach became bright red and the acid secretion increased. The doctors diverted him by joking about some things that had happened in the lab. With this diversion, Tom's stomach color and acidity returned to normal, but when the joking stopped and everyone was silent, Tom's stomach again became inflamed.

ANXIETY

Tom's stepdaughter was having a bladder examination to determine whether or not she had cancer. Tom experienced both doubt and dread over the possible outcome of the tests, and his stomach became red, more active, and secreted more acid. On another occasion, the experimenters were late arriving in the lab and Tom became anxious, thinking that perhaps he had made a mistake and was supposed to meet them someplace else. His stomach reacted as it had with his stepdaughter's tests — redness, hypersecretion, and hypermobility.

These and other experiments reflected Cannon's fight-or-flight findings. With emotions of hostility, resentment, anxiety, and chronic conflict, Tom's stomach showed "fight" reactions. This was true also with pleasurable thoughts of eating, which may represent primitive ideas of devouring one's enemies. In all these instances, Tom's stomach exhibited increased vascularity (redness), motility, and secretion. On the other hand, fear, sadness, and other feelings involving a desire for withdrawal or retreat showed a depression of gastric function (pallor, decreased motility, and decreased secretion). The changes were associated with appropriate variation in general bodily activity and talkativeness; sadness created silence and minimum movement.

Today, it is possible for a gastroenterologist to get a direct look at a patient's stomach by having the patient swallow a flexible gastroscope, which has a light at its end, but the chance to look at the stomach immediately during spontaneous emotional reactions hasn't reoccurred since Tom was studied.

SEVEN

Body Language

Even in the absence of speech, it is usually possible to judge the emotional state of another person when strong emotions are involved. Just walking down the street, we can notice people who are happy or sad or preoccupied or angry. That is because emotions almost always are **expressed** (pressed to the outside) and so are visible.

The most complete study of the way emotions are expressed was made by Charles Darwin, the author of *Origin of Species* and the originator of the Theory of Evolution. Although later investigators have added to these first studies of "**body language**," the original findings still hold true.

Most of the observations in this chapter were taken from Darwin's ground-breaking book, *The Expression of Emotions in Man and Animals*.

Darwin himself had been observing for 30 years the way in which emotions are expressed. He had looked carefully at animals and at infants; he had observed the insane because he believed they "are liable to the strongest passions and give uncontrolled vent to them"; he had showed photographs displaying various emotions to different observers to see how closely they could interpret the emotion. Finally, he had

51

studied the great masters of painting and sculpture, although he felt that because beauty was the objective, the works were often an incomplete representation of emotion. But Darwin had not been able to learn one critical and fundamental fact: Does the way emotions are expressed depend on race and culture or is there a universal way in which emotions are expressed?

To get the answer to this most important question, in 1867 Darwin sent inquiries to reliable observer friends living in different parts of the world — Australia, New Zealand, Borneo, the Malay archipelago, India, Ceylon (now Sri Lanka), Africa, and North and South America. He asked questions such as: Is astonishment expressed by the eyes and mouth being opened wide, and by the eyebrows being raised? When a man concentrates deeply on any subject, or tries to understand something that's puzzling him, does he frown, or does the skin beneath the lower eyelids become wrinkled? When someone is depressed, are the corners of the mouth lowered and is the inner corner of each eyebrow raised by that muscle which the French call the "grief muscle"?

When the answers came in, almost every question was answered in the affirmative, usually amplified by detailed comments describing the various actions and expressions. Darwin didn't trust a simple "yes" or "no" answer but the sum total of the responses added up to a resounding *yes*. Borneo Dyaks, Chinese living in the Malay, Atnah and Espyox tribes living in North America, Australian aborigines, Maoris in New Zealand, Englishmen in London all expressed emotions in the same manner; the language of emotions was indeed a universal one. It is consistent with this universality that Laura Dewey

Bridgman, the first blind deaf-mute person to be successfully educated in school, indicated "yes" with a nod and "no" with a shaking of the head before these actions could have been either acquired or learned by her, and she responded in the expected manner in other emotional situations as well.

These universal responses are seen when emotions *are* expressed, although there is tremendous individual variation in the intensity of expression. Observation teaches us a great deal about personality; we know, for instance, that one person will laugh at something another person will find completely unamusing. Often, too, emotions are experienced but not visibly expressed. Sometimes they are consciously **suppressed**. A good poker player never will reveal by a smile or other expression of emotion that he is holding a good hand. But again, the important contribution of Darwin's questions and the answers he received to them is that all over the world, the muscular responses of people when they *do* express their feelings are qualitatively similar.

Darwin's Observations

Usually, strong emotions are expressed verbally as well as by nonverbal body language. When we communicate with others we add to the words we are saying facial and other body expressions of the emotions experienced as we talk about them. The strongest verbal and nonverbal communication takes place when we are dealing directly with the emotional situation, rather than later when we are relating it to somebody. Our feelings are revealed not only by the words our voices are saying but by the sound of our voices. We raise our voices not only in anger but with many other emotions. When we are suffering, we often register our discomfort in high-pitched tones.

Sound itself without words conveys meaning. A belly laugh produces a noise quite different from that emitted under less humorous conditions. In the prolonged type of suffering known as **depression**, we sigh frequently. When we want to register contempt, we tend to blow out of our mouth or nostrils producing a "pooh" or "pish" sound.

Animal Behavior

In the animal kingdom as well, different sounds reflect different emotional states. Male animals use a variety of mating calls to entice the female. Animals emit sounds of despair, typified by the bleating of a ewe when one of its lambs is lost. With anger, lions roar and dogs growl and bark; it is interesting that while the bark of joy is similar to the bark of rage, the two sounds can be distinguished. Animals and large birds can stamp the ground to produce certain sounds, feathers can be ruffled, and the porcupine has certain hollow quills that are used to produce a continuous sound to warn away enemies. Along with specific sounds, involuntary erection of hairs and feathers takes place with anger or fear, especially when both emotions are felt. This makes the animal or bird appear larger and therefore more frightening to its enemies or rivals.

In observing the emotional responses of animals, Darwin noted behavior that serves no purpose now but had a function at one time. If a dog wants to go to sleep on the carpet, he turns round and round and scratches the carpet with his fore-paws; it's as if he intended to trample down the grass and dig a hollow in the same manner as his early ancestors probably did.

Darwin observed also that animals will completely reverse an inappropriate emotional expression the moment they discover that they've been mistaken. He cites the example of a man approaching a dog from a distance. The dog, thinking a potential enemy is coming toward him, gets into the traditional position for attack. He walks upright with his head slightly raised; his tail is held erect and quite rigid; his hair will bristle, especially the hairs along his neck and back; his pricked ears are directed forward, and his eyes have a fixed stare. Then, as he prepares to spring on his enemy ready to growl savagely, his canine teeth are uncovered and his ears are pressed backward on his head. But if he discovers that the man is his master rather than a stranger, the dog's whole bearing is reversed. His body sinks downward or he may even crouch; he lowers his tail and waves it from side to side; the hair on his body that had bristled immediately becomes smooth; his ears, while lowered and drawn backward, are not kept close to his head; his lips hang loosely and his eyes no longer are round and staring. He has quickly discovered that his initial fight-or-flight response no longer is needed and he now acts appropriately; different autonomic nervous system messages direct muscles to assume a friendly or servile posture. While the dog was used as an example, other animals have similar responses. When a cat hisses and arches its back, it is both frightened and angry; in this state, the cat can inflict injury on an intruder like an unfamiliar dog.

Specific Expressions of Emotion

Literature is filled with descriptions of emotional scenes because the interaction of feelings is what gives life to a story. Shakespeare has several excellent portrayals. Here is Juliet, embarrassed by what she considers an indiscreet admission, telling Romeo:

> Thou know'st the mask of night is on my face;
> Else would a maiden blush bepaint my cheek,
> For that which thou hast heard me speak tonight.

or we can listen to Caesar as he observes Cassius:

> Yond Cassius has a lean and hungry look;
> He thinks too much: such men are dangerous.

Malcolm in *Macbeth* advises that it is better to express than to suppress emotion:

> Give sorrow words; the grief that does not speak
> Whispers the o'er-fraught heart and bids it break.

or finally in *Henry V*, we can hear the Bard describing rage:

> But when the blast of war blows in our ears,
> Then imitate the action of the tiger:
> Stiffen the sinews, summon up the blood,
> Then lend the eye a terrible aspect;
> Now set the teeth, and stretch the nostril wide,
> Hold hard the breath, and bend up every spirit
> To his full height! On, on, you noblest English.

The universal expressions of specific and uncomplicated emotion can be noted either by observing others or by looking in a mirror as we simulate the emotions involved.

LAUGHTER

This is the most typical way of expressing joy or happiness. It evolves from smiling, and infants at an average age of 45 days begin to smile. During the act of laughing, the mouth is opened wide with its corners drawn upward and backward and because of increased circulation, the eyes appear brighter. (With depression or dehydration, in which there is decreased circulation, the eyes appear dull.)

There are many types of laughter caused by a wide variety of situations. The most relaxed type of laughter takes place when we feel happy. But while we laugh and joke when we feel good, we constantly use humor to relieve tension during stressful times. For example, soldiers just before a dangerous battle invariably wisecrack to try and show that they're not really afraid. Students do the same thing before important, anxiety-producing exams. We often use humor to mask disappointments, and we may joke to give the impression that being rejected in romance didn't really hurt or to show the outside world that we really weren't that disappointed over a job we didn't get. In instances like these, instead of doing what we feel like doing—hiding, running away, or crying—we cope by making light of the situation and figuratively we laugh with tears in our eyes.

The reason humans developed this quality of laughter relates to the process of civilization itself. The more civilized we are, the more we repress disturbing thoughts (remove them from the conscious part of our mind and keep them imprisoned in another part of our mind called the unconscious). This **repression** results in increased tension, and therefore civilized people have a greater need for mechanisms

like laughter that will relieve tension. It is an interesting fact
that the laughter of infants, who are uncivilized human beings,
is based on pleasant sensations and *not* on what we call a
"sense of humor." The sense of humor develops later, usually
about the time that a child begins to dream.

CRYING

The most visible manifestation of unhappiness, crying also
occurs during moments of great joy or relief. In the act of
crying, eye muscle contraction leads to drawing up of the
upper lip and if the mouth is open, drawing down of the
corners by depressor muscles. Crying gives relief from suffering in the same way as the agony of severe pain is relieved
by writhing of the body, grinding of the teeth, and shrieking.

Infants who are suffering from hunger or other discomfort
cry out and the blood vessels of the eye become engorged;
then reflex impulses are sent to the lachrymal glands, resulting
in the production of tears, while at the same time, the eye
muscles contract. The muscles of the eye contract not only
during screaming and sobbing but also while blowing the nose,
laughing, coughing, retching, vigorous scratching, and sneez-
ing. This contraction protects the delicate blood vessels of the
eye by limiting or preventing the blood vessel dilation (ex-
pansion of the blood vessel tube so that it carries more blood);
dilation, if unchecked, could result in hemorrhage of the eye
vessels.

Gradually we learn to produce tears over unhappy situations
without any other muscular actions. Among animals, Indian
elephants are the only ones who have been known to cry tears
when in despair.

EXPRESSIONS OF THE MOUTH

Determination is shown by closing the mouth firmly at the beginning of any violent or prolonged exertion or delicate operation. With determined concentration, breathing may be stopped temporarily and voluntarily to avoid distraction.

SHRUGGING THE SHOULDERS

Shrugging implies that the action we performed was unintentional or at least unavoidable, or it can indicate that we can't perform a certain action; furthermore, it can mean that we were unable to prevent the action just taken by another person. In these cases, it represents an apology of sorts. The gesture also can indicate patience or absence of any intention to resist. A decisive, big shrug may mean "I won't do it" instead of "I can't do it."

BLUSHING

The tendency to blush is inherited and the blushing occurs most often on exposed areas of the body, usually the face, ears, and neck, areas richly supplied with capillary circulation. These areas are subject to frequent changes resulting from the dilation and contraction of blood vessels. Blushing occurs with shyness, modesty, shame, and embarrassment, and confusion often accompanies it. Blushing, like many other manifestations of emotion, must have had a protective function originally but whatever it was has been lost during the evolution of civilization. Self-consciousness is a feature of all emotional situations that cause blushing and with these emotions, there is an attempt to hide or to avoid looking at others. Shy or ashamed children avoid observation by burying their heads in their mothers' dresses or by throwing themselves face down in their mothers' laps. A parent's reprimand for shyness under these circumstances causes completely the reverse of what is intended; by this criticism, *more* attention is focused on the child who in turn becomes even more self-conscious.

VARIATIONS IN BREATHING AND CLENCHED FISTS

With the extreme anger that is rage, the face becomes red or almost purple, the veins on the forehead and neck become distended, the chest heaves, and the nostrils dilate. The head and body are protruded in a gesture of challenge. The expressions "breathing out vengeance" and "fuming with anger" are accurate; sharp breaths of anger are taken, between which the mouth is firmly closed, showing determination. Sometimes the lips are protruded like the apes but more often, they are retracted to reveal clenched teeth. The fists (in many parts of the world) are clenched and the enraged person acts as if he wants to hit or push away an offender. Clenched fists have a cultural origin; they are characteristic only of those regions where fighting with the fists is usual.

SNEERING

In this characteristic expression, one upper lip is raised to expose the canine tooth on that side. The face is a little up-turned and half-turned away from the person at the receiving end of the sneer. The sneer is similar to the snarl of a dog. Our primitive ancestors had prominent canine teeth and used them to bite during fighting. When we sneer, we are making a weak symbolic gesture of strength.

Nonspecific Expressions of Emotions

Rather than employing direct gestures that specifically result from discrete emotions, the expression of complex emotions like hatred and love involves multiple and varied actions.

Love. When a mother holds a baby, she usually smiles affectionately. There is a strong desire to touch and be touched by those for whom we feel a strong bond; dogs and cats enjoy rubbing against their owners, and cats purr contentedly when rubbed or scratched on their abdomens. Hand-holding and mutual caresses are characteristic of lovers. So is kissing, but this is not an innate sign of love and affection. Kissing is unknown in several parts of the world and replaced by rubbing noses in the case of Eskimos or by blowing on various parts of the body or by patting the arms, breasts, or stomach, or in some areas by one man striking his own face with the hands or feet of another.

Tender feelings are complex and comprise affection, joy, and sympathy. Often when thinking of a loved one who is away, we sympathize with ourselves when thoughts of happier times contrast with our present state of mind. Reunions with loved ones frequently bring tears, which may be in part tears of joy and gratitude but may also be the result of brief thoughts of the grief that would have occurred had the reunion been prevented. After a loss in the family, reunions of surviving family members are usually highly emotional because the precious nature of the love that binds them together has been tragically emphasized.

Hatred. Prolonged reflection about a hated person will frequently evoke the reaction of rage unless that person seems insignificant to us. In that case, we experience only contempt or disdain. But it is possible to feel hatred without any physical expression of that hatred. Unlike what happens with the kind of anger provoked in a violent confrontation, hatred can be a slow-burning emotion that can be overtly suppressed, either partially or totally. The slogan "don't get mad, get even" has been used by some to proclaim that when one has been unjustly treated, energy should be used effectively rather than wasted with a display of anger.

Like love and hatred, there are other emotions in which the state of mind produced is complex and not always expressed in a manner fixed enough to be recognized. Jealousy, envy, avarice, suspicion, guilt, ambition, pride, and humility are examples of emotions often difficult for an observer to pinpoint.

It's easy to see why overt body responses are important and often dramatic indicators of a person's emotional state. But less obvious, subtle body signals also are used to express emotion. These fascinating signals, discovered and studied only in recent years, are discussed in the next chapter.

EIGHT

Modern Body Language

Our bodies respond to our emotions by sending out signals that others can "read." We can learn more about someone by observing how his or her body is reacting than from what he or she is *saying*. Newer studies have extended the science of body language to include subtle and largely unconscious uses of nonverbal communication. This new science, **kinesics**, which began after the end of World War II, has grown steadily and is now being studied at most academic centers.

The chief functions of body language are providing information to others, exercising social control (which includes protection of territory), and expressing intimacy. Social control involves deciding the appropriate physical distance that should be maintained during social relationships, whether at a party or alone with someone. Intimacy means physical and emotional closeness. We are the least intimate with strangers, slightly more with acquaintances, still more with casual friends, and the most intimate with family and close friends.

Emotions are revealed by both conscious and unconscious actions. Making a fist may be either a conscious act or an unconscious one; on the other hand, an entirely unconscious

63

action takes place when something pleasant is viewed — the pupil of the eye enlarges. Some of these gestures, postures, facial expressions, and other methods of nonverbal communication have been inherited, whereas others have been learned.

The meanings of the more recently observed subtle actions are not universal; they depend heavily on environment. In our culture, for example, avoiding someone's gaze most often indicates shyness or guilt, but when a young Puerto Rican avoids someone's gaze, he or she simply is showing respect for the other person.

Symbolic gestures are a recognized nonverbal way of giving information in a rapid way. These gestures, unlike unconscious body movements, usually are known to both the person using the gesture and to the recipient. We may shake a fist at someone, make a V-for-victory sign or an everything's-O.K. sign by holding up the hand and forming a circle with the thumb and index finger, stick out our tongues to show derision, or whirl our index finger in a circle close to our head to indicate that an idea or a person is crazy. We all can think of many, many more of these recognized gestures, which share one common feature: they can be easily put into words. But the gesture is quicker, more direct, and usually leaves a more vivid impression. This brings out an important point: All nonverbal communication really is saying in actions what either we consciously or unconsciously want to express in words. Body language often contradicts verbal language. A person may be saying "yes" while at the same time his or her head is moving back and forth in a "no" gesture. When this happens, believe the body language rather than the words. Body language never lies.

We communicate nonverbally primarily by the use of touch,

posture, and gaze. Depending on the situation, touch is used to show several different emotions. If we gently touch the hand or face or other parts of the body of someone who is in pain emotionally or physically, we are expressing sympathy for that person, letting him or her know without speaking a word that we too understand the hurt that is being felt and that we feel sorry about it. Then again, touch can be used to show friendship. Putting an arm around someone can communicate warmth in a way that no words possibly can express. (Of course, there are some people who don't like to be touched ever or only by the most intimate friends or members of the family. Putting an arm around such a person may elicit a different kind of reaction — a stiffening of the body and a withdrawal that sends a clear message.)

Touch, in addition to much individual variation, is also influenced by culture. North and South Americans and Mediterranean peoples generally touch more; other nationalities, such as the British, are more reserved and while our presidents often put their arms around their friends, it's unlikely you'll see the Queen of England being publicly on the giving or receiving end of such demonstrative behavior. Similarly, Americans doing business in Japan have had to learn about cultural differences. For example, enthusiastic slapping on the back is considered poor manners in Japan. "Japanese appreciate restraint (enryo), like a tiger who hides his claws, rather than outward expressions of emotion," a Japanese business consultant states, adding that mutual dependence (amae) is a sign of trust rather than weakness in Japan. Being asked to do a favor in that country is an honor. An American attorney who deals with Japanese companies also stresses the importance of body language. "The Japanese consider meeting you, getting information from you *and watching how you behave with them* at least as important as the economic terms of the deal that you are going to strike with them," he advises.

Touch also plays an important role in romance. Here the message conveyed varies from affectionate hand-holding to sexual signals that request more intimate contact. Each situation is different, and both males and females have to determine what is appropriate and what isn't.

Body language is frequently used to acknowledge the rules of territory. Territory in this connection means space, and everyone has a need for some personal space. Birds stake out their territories by certain birdcalls that warn outsiders to keep clear, and larger species of animals also stake out territories that they mark as their own. Humans are not exceptions, and we require a certain amount of space to feel comfortable or secure. The amount of space we need varies with the intimacy of the relationship. We feel completely comfortable being physically close to family members, but in other situations — walking down the street, standing on the subway, riding in an elevator — we use body language to maintain our social distance.

We can't avoid riding in crowded buses or subways if we live in the city, but when we sit or stand, we consciously make an effort to avoid contact with fellow passengers who are not acquaintances. If five strangers are riding in an elevator, they often will distribute themselves symmetrically, using the four corners with the fifth person taking the center, like five dots on a die; each is staking out his or her own space while simultaneously respecting the space of the other passengers. If someone moves in close when there is room to do otherwise, the person whose space has been invaded reacts with body language of displeasure and uneasiness by stiffening up, tapping a foot, or other gestures.

Territory often is acknowledged by glancing or gazing at another person. When two people approach each other from opposite directions in the street, as the distance between them closes to about eight feet, each person looks away before passing. This is an unconscious mutual acknowledgment of territory; each is in effect saying with that avoiding glance, "I'm sorry to be infringing on your territory but it can't be helped."

Staring is impolite, but it often gives a clue about how a person doing the staring feels. Just as two people in a restaurant who consider themselves superior may talk in loud voices that show that the conversations of other diners are unimportant and need not be considered, so too does staring indicate a similar attitude. Some individuals, unduly impressed with themselves, may stare at someone as if the other person were an object rather than a human being with feelings. This kind of stare seems to say: "I am looking at a nonperson and I have every right to stare as long as this object holds any interest for me."

Status is confirmed by the use of space. The higher the rank of an executive in a company, the larger the office, and everyone in the company is aware of this fact. When called to the office of the president of his company, a junior executive won't walk right up to the boss's desk; instead, "Junior" will stand deferentially at the door until invited in. But the vice-president will walk directly into that office and take a seat. This action, along with the accompanying relaxed state, is body language that gives the message: "I'm almost as important in this company as you are. We both recognize that we relate as close associates rather than as employee-boss." Space is required not only by those who wish to assert status but also by introverted persons, those personalities who concentrate on the "inner self." **Introverts**, because of this absorption with inner thoughts and fantasies, feel insecure in close situations; the outside world is less familiar to them. On the other hand, **extroverts**, outgoing people whose interests focus on objects and actions of the outside world, require and desire far less space.

The protocol of behavior in the presence of royalty involves body language; when the custom of bowing and curtseying began, it was analagous to a weaker dog lying on its stomach as a sign of submission to a stronger dog.

Investigators have studied many other body language responses. For instance, when another's advances or attempts at familiarity make us feel uncomfortable and we wish to resist this intrusion, we cross our arms and legs, thus "closing off" our bodies; however at other times, the same action — crossing our legs — may represent a relaxed state. Body language clearly varies with different situations, and in order to accurately evaluate someone else's body language, we must know the circumstances that evoked an action.

When we converse, we continuously use body language of which we're unaware. If an answer is expected when we have finished speaking, our head, hands, and eyelids make upward movements, whereas they move downward after we have made a statement that doesn't require an answer.

Posture is important in showing how a person feels. We all have seen the body language of depression; the entire body sags, the abdomen relaxes, and the stomach protrudes. This appearance sharply contrasts with the erect stance of someone feeling confident.

There are hundreds of body language responses to situations involving emotions. Close observation of people in different situations will reveal the meaning of nonverbal actions, provided the circumstances inducing the behavior also are appreciated. These observations are fascinating, and in addition they yield valuable understanding of the various emotional states we encounter in ourselves and others.

NINE

Emotions, Stress, and the Body

In 1925, a Montreal medical student, Hans Selye, observed a curious phenomenon. His professor was showing the class several patients with different diseases and was interested only in the specific manifestations of each disease. Yet, all these patients showed certain things in common — weight loss or fever, aches and pains, an enlarged spleen or liver and various other nonspecific signs and symptoms — all of which Selye's professor found unimportant. But to the young medical student, these nonspecific signs and symptoms of what he termed "the **syndrome** of just being sick" were the important parts of the illness, **stress**, to which he was to devote his entire scientific life.

After years of experimentation, Sclye defined stress as "the rate of all the wear and tear caused by life." He discovered the kinds of physical damage that stress produces and determined how the body defends itself against this injury. He named this defense the **general adaptation syndrome** (GAS).

Disease is caused by many factors, including emotional stress (sustained, damaging emotional response). Genetic (inherited) factors are the sole cause of diseases like hemophilia, and they also play a partial role in illnesses like heart disease. Environmental factors, such as air pollutants, food unhealthful for us, adverse weather conditions, insufficient exercise, etc., can cause disease. Infections—bacterial, viral, parasitic, fungus—are diseases primarily of the environment, although our natural body defenses—**host resistance**—play an important role and may be affected by emotions.

When thinking about the cause of disease, it is important to remember that a *single* factor rarely is responsible; more often there are multiple causes.

Emotions are the primary cause of some diseases, whereas in others, their role is fragmentary and often questionable. But aside from the question of causation, there always is an emotional response to serious illness, depression being the most prominent feature.

Emotional Stress

Stress is derived from the word *distress* and means an unpleasant feeling of pressure. It is produced either by the overload of too many emotions at once or by anxiety from a single but very worrisome source.

The reactions to stress are individual. Some people welcome stress and actually seek it out because they feel better working under pressure. These personalities, working in high-pressure jobs, become ill when they go on vacation. They find relaxing on a beach intolerable and develop headaches, stomachaches, and the like. We can see that stress stimuli are harmful only when a person *perceives* them as noxious. And when these stimuli are felt to be too uncomfortable, they are moved into the unconscious to avoid awareness of them.

Any disease caused mainly by emotional factors is called **psychosomatic**. The word is a combination of two Greek words — *psyche* meaning soul or spirit and *soma* meaning body.

While reading these descriptions, remember that the role of emotion varies from disease to disease. In alcoholism and anorexia nervosa, emotion is the most important factor while in asthma, allergy is responsible primarily for the symptoms. The part that emotion plays in any psychosomatic disease varies from person to person. Thus emotion may be an important factor in some people with asthma while in others it may be of minor importance.

Emotions are known to affect the immune system, a fact being taken into account by researchers who believe that suppression of emotion plays a partial role in causing several diseases, including cancer.

Psychosomatic Diseases

ACNE

A universal skin disorder affecting adolescents, **acne** is caused by oversecretion of the fatty lubricating material, sebum, which plugs the ducts of the sebaceous glands. The plugging-up causes whiteheads and blackheads that often become infected. Sex hormones first produced at puberty are needed for the development of acne; the condition does not occur without the presence of active ovaries or testes. Researchers studied several young people and carefully measured the amount of sebum they produced over a two-week period. The amount of sebum secreted and the number of pustules increased markedly when there was anger.

ALCOHOLISM

Alcoholism, an addiction to alcohol, is the third major health problem in the United States. Children, even those of elementary-school age, are its victims as well as adults. There is only one cure for alcoholism: the alcoholic must stop drinking.

Physical causative factors include a hereditary disposition to the disease. Children of alcoholic parents have a much greater chance of becoming alcoholics, even when they are adopted at birth into a family where no alcoholism exists. Alcoholics may lack certain chemical substances in the body whose absence may cause them to react to alcohol differently from the nonalcoholic; because alcoholics often have low blood sugars, it is possible that they break down carbohydrates differently from the way other people do.

Intense emotional disturbances frequently trigger the onset of alcoholism. Once the disease begins, the alcoholic fails to recognize that anxiety is a limited condition; instead of living with the anxiety or working out its causes and alleviating them if possible, the alcoholic uses drink to "blot out" worries. Soon drinking becomes the way to avoid the pain of emotional problems. These problems don't go away, however. They only seem to because the alcohol interferes with the thinking process. But despite this thinking "anesthesia," alcoholics do experience unbelievable psychological discomfort and even in a drunken stupor hear and remember unpleasant things that may be said about them. As the disease progresses, their self-image becomes damaged because they are aware of the hurt they are inflicting on themselves and their families.

Once drinking has started and has become excessive, two major emotional changes become a prominent part of alcoholic behavior. The first is denial. The alcoholic refuses to admit to himself or herself or to others that a drinking problem exists. "I can stop anytime I want to" is the rationalization. Second, the alcoholic begins to separate himself from the society around him, progressively withdrawing from family and friends. This lonely process is called **alienation**, and eventually drinking companions are the only "friends" the alcoholic has. The process works in reverse as well; not only does the alcoholic do the cutting off, but friends and acquaintances stop seeing this person who has become difficult and embarrassing. Drinking always leads to family problems, and sometimes a wife or husband may decide to leave an alcoholic spouse. Children suffer greatly from the presence of an alcoholic in the home and a national organization, ALATEEN, a division of Alcoholics Anonymous (AA), is a fellowship group for teen-aged sons and daughters of alcoholics. Group discussions help young people learn effective ways to cope with problems related to having an alcoholic family member.

EATING DISORDERS

Anorexia nervosa is mostly a disease of adolescence, characterized by a rapid loss of weight caused by extreme dieting. Usually, it appears in a young woman who has become obsessed by the concept that she is overweight or even obese. The weight she believes to be ideal is much lower than that of her peers. The disease is found most commonly in young white women of middle-to-upper socioeconomic classes. For

example, a study at the University of California at Los Angeles
Neuropsychiatric Institute included 86 white females of mid-
dle-to-high socioeconomic status, whose ages ranged from 13
to 21, with a mean age of 17.

The first report of anorexia nervosa was published in France
in 1789. E. Naudeau, who reported this case of a young girl
who died from "an extraordinary aversion to food," noted that
something was wrong in the relationship between the girl and
her mother. Today, the relationship of the anorexic patient
to her family is considered an important factor in the disease.

There are some characteristic attitudes and symptoms that
patients with anorexia exhibit. The UCLA group found that
body dissatisfaction, pursuit of thinness, and overactivity were
general characteristics in anorexia nervosa.

Looking for this thin "ideal" is widespread today, and its
danger is realized only when a celebrity such as Karen Car-
penter tragically dies from the disease. If you look at pictures
of women models, you will discover that a high percentage
of them are significantly underweight and appear to have anorexia.

There are some physical changes that accompany anorexia
nervosa. Menarche may not occur if the disease starts early;
in other cases involving severe weight loss and malnutrition,
menstrual periods stop. Hormonal changes are responsible for
this and other physical signs, such as hypothyroidism. There
is a reduction in hypothalamic, pituitary, adrenal, and ovarian
hormones (decreased estrogen, for example). This generalized
reduction is thought to be secondary to the starvation state.

In the emotional realm of the disease, depression seems to
be a prominent manifestation. Some are depressed before the
onset of symptoms, whereas other patients become second-

arily depressed after they have begun to regain weight (probably because they have had to give up their pursuit of the thinness they had in mind). No lack of appetite is present. Indeed, there seems to be an obsession with food, but the discipline and suffering needed for voluntary starvation appears to the patient to give her a "control" over her life that previously she never felt she had.

The anorexic patient often feels that she owes something to her parents, whom she has perceived as giving her more than she "deserves." She feels unworthy because she isn't living up to her parents' "expectations" and feels in danger of losing her parents' love. The starvation makes her feel "special." It is evident that anorexia nervosa is not simply an illness of weight and appetite; its essence is a lack of self-confidence. **Behavior modification** (*see* Chapter 11), in which gain of weight is rewarded and failure to gain punished, won't work in anorexia. Although the patient may succeed in gaining weight under this treatment, the basic disorder remains. Unless the psychological problems are tackled, understood, and faced, the patient will relapse. Because malnutrition interferes with the ability to think and reason clearly, some weight gain must take place before **psychotherapy** (*see* Chapter 10) becomes effective.

Once an anorexic patient understands the reasons why she has had such a poor self-image and accepts her body size as normal, she frequently describes to the therapist the horror and suffering of her starvation ordeal.

There is another eating disorder called **bulimia** that is closely associated with anorexia nervosa, in that emotional disturbances precede both conditions. This disorder is characterized by periodic eating binges which, to the bulimic, seem to be

to get rid of something or to dispose of too heavy an emotional load. Often, the episodes of diarrhea are followed by periods of constipation. The disease is not serious, and while there is no specific treatment, various antidiarrheal, antispasmodic, and tranquilizer drugs are helpful. Sometimes counseling or psychotherapy is indicated.

Ulcerative colitis is the most serious chronic disease of the colon. Emotional stress is thought to be a definite factor in its development and flare-ups. It is characterized by ulcers of the rectum or colon or both, and diarrhea and rectal bleeding are frequent beginning signs of the disease. The severity of ulcerative colitis varies widely.

CORONARY ARTERY DISEASE

The heart, the muscular pump that is responsible for pushing the blood throughout the body, is itself nourished by blood vessels called the coronary arteries. When these arteries get partially plugged by deposits of cholesterol and other fatty substances, which in combination with calcium form gritty plaques, less blood flows through these arteries and **coronary artery disease** results. When the heart has to perform extra work during exercise, during cold and windy weather, or during times of great emotional stress, the diminished circulation from partially plugged vessels results in the heart muscle being deprived of enough oxygen to fulfill its needs; the result is a kind of squeezing chest pain called **angina pectoris**. (The word *angina* is derived from the Greek and means strangling). If the arterial plugging is severe enough, that person may suffer a heart attack (which also is called a coronary or **myocardial infarction**). (There is frequent confusion about heart attack and heart failure. They are different entities; heart failure is the condition that results from the heart's not working properly as a pump, usually caused by weakening of the heart muscle.)

Like so many diseases, many factors in combination cause heart attacks; how much each factor contributes still is not known today. Heredity, diet, exercise, smoking, overweight, blood pressure all play a role as does emotion, a factor more and more acknowledged as being important both in causing coronary artery disease and in the development of symptoms once the disease is present.

The role of emotion in causing his own heart symptoms was recognized by the great English surgeon, John Hunter. He knew that an anginal attack could be brought on if a coachman was late or if a servant neglected to follow orders he had given. He observed that emotions like joy or sadness had no effect, but anger, anxiety, or even minor irritations could precipitate the chest pain. He understood how precarious was his situation and proclaimed that "my life is in the hands of any rascal who chooses to annoy and tease me." And Hunter's prediction came to pass. During a staff meeting at St. George's Hospital, he became furious with two physicians and abruptly left the meeting. Just outside the door, he suddenly groaned and fell to the floor dead.

Approximately 30 years ago, researchers began to study the role of personality in the causation of coronary artery disease. Today, the concept that emotional factors contribute to the *development* of coronary artery disease has received general acceptance although the exact nature of the personality factors involved has not been resolved. Some believe that time consciousness, overwhelming ambition, and extreme impatience are the primary contributory factors (Personality Type A), while other investigators feel that the patient's repression of emotion and denial of the existence of any emotional problems are more important contributors. Regardless of the specific factors, the effect of emotional stress and strain is now taken into account by almost all heart disease researchers (along with heredity, diet, exercise, etc.) as an important causative factor when coronary artery disease is present.

As mentioned, many factors contribute to the development of coronary artery disease, but one study is particularly fascinating. The Italian-American community of Roseto, Pennsylvania, was the subject of an intensive research project in 1964. Despite subjects being overweight, eating a high-fat and high-cholesterol diet, not exercising enough, etc., their rate of heart attack incidence was significantly lower than that of other communities, and this was attributed to the relaxed and unrepressed personalities of the residents of Roseto.

HEADACHE

If it were possible to chart all the **headaches** that occur all over the world, one dramatic fact would be evident: almost all of them are caused by tension! True, a percentage are the result of organic diseases like brain tumors or head trauma or sinus problems, but compared with psychological causes, that percentage is minuscule. So when we develop a headache, it's almost always at a time when we've been worrying about something or when we've been under a great deal of stress. Headaches often run in families so that children of parents who complain frequently about headaches are more likely to have them than those whose parents rarely suffer from this kind of discomfort. In addition to tension headaches, there is another type of headache, vascular or migraine, which has a strong hereditary component and which, although caused by many factors, is often precipitated by tension.

Tension headache. This extremely common type of headache occurs under stressful conditions that require prolonged concentration such as cramming for exams, driving in heavy traffic, and countless other stressful states. Tension headaches most often feel as if a tight band were squeezing the head, although sometimes these headaches are pounding in character. They are most often caused by contraction of the muscles attached to the occiput, the back part of the skull.

Migraine headaches. These headaches are caused by dilation of one of the external blood vessels of the head and usually involve one half of the head. They occur in susceptible individuals after periods of intense striving with unsatisfying results. Migraines can also be brought on by taking oral contraceptives and other drugs, by menstrual periods, by missed meals, and by other factors, but stress remains the most important cause; those subject to this very painful type of headache have what is described as perfectionistic and inflexible personalities, marked by insecurity and resentment. Often, they have a dread of being found wrong.

HYPERTENSION

Hypertension is high blood pressure, the most common type of which is called essential hypertension. Although there are many exceptions, those with essential hypertension are thought to be people who are psychologically poised for combat and whose aggression is unconsciously restrained. Narrowing of small arteries (arterioles) causes increased resistance to blood flow, and this in turn causes a rise in blood pressure.

People with essential hypertension seem to be preparing themselves for blood loss. In other words, they're physiologically ready for "fight," but they never act it out and they avoid asserting themselves.

During the 1942–1943 siege of Leningrad, the incidence of hypertension climbed from 4.1 percent to 64 percent, a staggering increase. In contrast to soldiers in the field, these Russian citizens were unable to fight against the enemy during this time. Another example of the role of stress was described when hypertension appeared in one of identical 20-year-old twin girls; the twin with high blood pressure was lighter in weight at birth, slower in growth, had more infections, was less outgoing, learned less easily, and was less capable of evoking love than was her twin. She felt like an "also-ran," and while she never asserted herself, she was constantly striving to equal the success of her sister.

ULCERS

Stress causes spasm of the muscles of the stomach and small intestine along with increased stomach acidity; if prolonged, this combination of acid and spasm eats away a portion of the lining of the stomach or first part of the small intestine (duodenum), leaving a painful, rounded eroded area called a **peptic ulcer**. We've all heard of the "ulcer type," a hard-driving worrier. Researchers offer a logical explanation for people with ulcer personalities: When faced with stressful situations, ulcer sufferers manufacture a great deal of stomach acid so that they can devour their enemies.

It is not hard for the ulcer victim to recognize the stressful

conditions that brought on the ulcer. Predictably, the incidence of ulcers has increased in women as they have taken
on jobs that in former times were open only to men.

There are many less serious psychosomatic disorders, such
as hyperventilation, cardiospasm (tightening of the esophagus), certain disturbances of heart rhythm (some types of rapid
heartbeats), fluid retention, hypoglycemia (low blood sugar),
and some types of hives and eczema.

Today, along with improved medical treatment, there is
increased awareness of the emotional stresses that produce
diseases or make them worse. With this knowledge and with
the ability to make appropriate changes in our behavior, we
have the tools to halt or diminish the severity of many stress-
caused diseases or better still, to prevent their occurrence.

TEN

Opening a Locked Door

We are living in a time when we can get effective help for emotional disturbances that persist over a long period and cause us much pain. **Psychiatrists** or clinical **psychologists** — professionals specializing in the diagnosis and treatment of emotional disorders — have had the training and experience to offer this help. This is fortunate for us because it is only relatively recently — this century in fact — that treatment has become available to us.

Emotional disturbances always are unpleasant, but those severe psychological and organic disorders that are associated with striking changes in behavior are devastating. Imagine what it was like for people who suffered from the very worst emotional upsets before help was available. Labeled "insane," in addition to suffering the agony of being unable to function in society, they were placed in chains in order to keep them "harmless." That was what happened until Philippe Pinel became chief physician, first at the Bicêtre and then at the Salpetriere, two famous mental hospitals in Paris. In 1795, Dr. Pinel ordered all chains and shackles removed from the women who were hospitalized at those institutions, thus inaugurating a new era in the treatment of emotional disease. Not only did he unchain patients, some of whom had been fettered for 40 years, but he also abolished worthless and uncomfortable treatments that were then in vogue — blistering, purging, and bleeding. He directed that patients be given sunny rooms, be permitted to exercise, and be treated with kindness. Many skeptics predicted that these radical steps would endanger the staff as well as the patients themselves, but Pinel's methods worked. The patients responded to his kindness and trust and while they seldom were cured, they were happier with their new freedom, and consequently their behavior improved. Because Pinel's humane methods were effective, they were adopted everywhere.

Pinel's contribution of compassionate care was a giant step forward, but a full century was to pass before the tenets of psychiatric treatment as we know it today, were discovered and instituted.

The man whose pioneering studies form the basis of modern psychiatry was a Viennese physician, Sigmund Freud. Known now as the father of psychotherapy, the specialty that deals with the treatment of emotional disorders, he developed a new technique called **psychoanalysis**, which today is one of the forms of psychotherapy. Before Freud, mental illness could be diagnosed and labeled but there was no effective way to *treat* it. Every disease of the mind was assumed to be caused by some physical abnormality — often a brain tumor or injury — and the available treatment was primitive, being limited to drugs, the soothing effect of water (hydrotherapy), or stimulation of the body with a mild electric current (electrotherapy). A. A. Brill, who brought psychoanalysis to America, recalled those early days: "When the patient was excited, he received some sedative; if he was depressed and felt fatigue, he was given a tonic; and when drugs failed, electricity or cold baths were recommended. All these remedies gave only temporary alleviation."

From the time when he first began to publish his findings, Freud was vilified and shunned by most of the Viennese medical community. Later, as his ideas were spread by his students, criticism of Freud was voiced by outraged alienists (an older, now obsolete word for psychiatrists) all over Europe. This was partly because new ideas invariably are resisted by those accustomed to doing things in the same old way. In Freud's case, there was another strong reason for rejection of his concepts: In the course of treating his patients, he discovered that buried sexual thoughts dating back to infancy often were responsible for emotional disturbances. In those days, any discussion of sexual problems of adults was upsetting enough, but Freud's studies had proven that sexual feelings were not confined to adults but rather, began in infancy and continued throughout life. "I treated my discoveries as ordinary contributions to science and hoped that others would treat them the same way," Freud recalled in 1914. "But the silence which followed my lectures, the void that was formed around my person, and the insinuations directed at me, made me realize gradually that statements concerning the role of sexuality in the etiology of the neuroses cannot hope to be treated like other communications. I realized that I belonged to those who 'have disturbed the world's sleep,' and that I could not count upon being treated objectively and with toleration." He added that he was prepared to "accept the fate which sometimes accompanies such discoveries."

Freud's insights into fundamental emotional disturbances

began when an older friend of his, Dr. Josef Breuer, told him about the case of a young woman whose **hysteria** he had cured. Breuer, from 1880 to 1882, had treated the woman by inducing a trance state called **hypnosis**. While hypnotized, the woman was able to recall disturbing incidents and fantasies that up to then had remained buried in her mind. Each time she was awakened from the hypnotic trance, physical symptoms disappeared as a result of this "talking cure." Painful, repressed memories had been exorcized.

Freud traveled to Paris in 1885 and spent a year studying with the famous French neurologist, Jean Martin Charcot. He witnessed and was impressed by Charcot's cures of hysteria through the use of suggestion made while the patient was hypnotized. Once Freud began to use Breuer's technique, he realized that talking about conflicts while the patient was under hypnosis was "much more attractive than the monotonous and violent suggestive command which was devoid of every possibility of inquiry."

Freud soon found that he was unable to hypnotize every patient, and thinking that his technique was to blame, he traveled again to France, this time to Nancy, to consult with two physicians who were experts in hypnosis — Drs. A. A. Liebault and Hippolyte Bernheim. He brought along one of those patients whom he couldn't hypnotize and Dr. Bernheim, after several attempts, was no more successful than Freud had been in achieving the state of hypnosis. The weeks spent with Bernheim, however, stimulated Freud's desire to investigate more thoroughly those troublesome emotional forces he found so fascinating.

When Freud returned to Vienna from France, he began to

test Breuer's "talking cure" on his own patients. In 1893, Freud and Breuer combined their cases and published the results of their studies. They called their treatment of investigation under hypnosis the cathartic method because, justifiably, they were convinced that its effectiveness depended upon **catharsis** — the bringing to the surface from areas of the brain where they had remained unconscious very disturbing emotional **conflicts**. Conflicts are caused by thoughts or feelings that pull in opposite directions; one part of us may say: "yes, I want to do this thing" while at the same time other thoughts (for different reasons) say: "no, I don't want to do this thing." Essentially, catharsis is purging, getting rid of something by making it surface. Once a painful conflict held in the unconscious is released, it becomes conscious and can be worked out (resolved) by making a decision about the best course of action. Now the previously buried conflict is understood and the patient feels freer and happier.

Because of his busy general medical practice, Dr. Breuer wondered whether he could afford to spend the time that his psychiatric investigations demanded. Moreover, as he began to probe deeper and deeper into the minds of his patients, he found that the process itself was disturbing his own emotional balance. Hence, Breuer decided to abandon the field. Not Freud! Irrevocably involved in the new territory he was exploring, he continued on alone.

Soon Freud made a fundamental discovery. He remembered back to the days with Bernheim and recalled a certain experiment that was designed to overcome posthypnotic amnesia. In that experiment, the patient could remember absolutely nothing that had taken place during the hypnosis when first awakened, but when he was urged to try and recall what had been said to him, eventually he was able to remember everything. Now, with patients he was unable to hypnotize, Freud used a variation of that experiment. He instructed those patients to tell him everything that came into their heads even if they considered the thought to be unimportant or irrelevant. He told them to avoid conscious reflection and instead to freely relate everything that spontaneously came to mind. Thus was born the process of **free association**, although Freud quickly discovered that these associations weren't really "free" at all; rather, they were tied to other buried material that had to be brought to the surface and analyzed. He gave the name psychoanalysis to this process.

Freud gradually gave up hypnotism as he further developed his technique of psychoanalysis, but he was always grateful for the lessons hypnosis had taught him; he understood that it was the first key he found that would unlock the unconscious and declared that "psychoanalysis is the administrator of the estate left by hypnotism."

Until 1902, Freud worked alone, but in that year he participated in the formation of a small group of Viennese physicians that met regularly at his home to learn and discuss the new technique. This was the first of many psychoanalytic study groups and each year, more and more new psychiatrists became members of these societies. The movement first gained international recognition in 1907 when a renowned Swiss physician, Professor Eugen Bleuler, contacted Freud and informed him that psychoanalysis was being studied at the Clinic of Psychiatry in Zurich. Carl Jung was a young physician at that clinic. He was to become one of the most famous psychoanalysts in the world. Initially, he was an enthusiastic disciple of Freud but later he became one of several psychiatrists who disagreed with Freud's concepts and split away from his teachings. Alfred Adler and Otto Rank were two other well-known psychoanalysts who defected from the Freudian viewpoint. Freud maintained that the unpopular sexual emphasis of his theories made it more comfortable for these men to pursue a different direction. This judgment may have been too harsh, however. Maturing students throughout history have developed ideas independent of and different from those of their teachers. As a result of the Swiss psychoanalysts' communications, the first psychoanalytic congress was held in 1908 at Salzburg, Austria, and the first psychoanalytic journal was founded under the editorship of Carl Jung.

Then, in 1909, a very prestigious invitation was issued to Freud and Jung. It came from the eminent psychologist G. Stanley Hall, who was president of Clark University in Worcester, Massachusetts. He asked the two men to travel to America and give several lectures to celebrate the university's twentieth anniversary. Freud was astonished to learn that not only were the professors at Clark familiar with his psychoanalytic papers but that they were teaching this new specialty in their classes. More importantly, Freud made two lifelong friends — the English psychiatrist Ernest Jones, who at that time was teaching at Toronto, and James J. Putnam, teacher of neuropathology at Harvard, who earlier had belittled psychoanalysis but later became its advocate. Jones, Freud's most eminent biographer, on returning home to London introduced psychoanalysis in England, thus performing the same task that A. A. Brill undertook in the United States. Within two decades of those Worcester lectures, psychoanalysis was established throughout the world.

Basic Concepts of Psychoanalysis

Freud states that there is one fundamental theory that is the "pillar upon which the edifice of psychoanalysis rests" and that is repression, the burying of unpleasant thoughts and emotions in the unconscious. Although buried, they cause symptoms, and in bringing them to the surface, two principles of therapy must be considered: **transference** and **resistance**. In transference, the patient transfers to the therapist the emotional attachments that existed in early life; essentially, the patient repeats the relationship he or she had with parents, feeling toward the therapist the same loves and hates he or she experienced toward the parents while growing up. Since this transference influences the patient's free association, it provides the therapist with valuable clues to conflicts. (When painful emotional areas are reached, the patient — rather than being able to free associate — "blocks" and remains silent. Now the therapist knows that the subject being explored is painful and filled with conflicts.) The patient, because transference has caused the same dependency on the therapist as existed with parents, cannot at first state the conflict. He or she has used much energy to keep these conflicts buried and has strong resistance to their being released. The patient reasons: "I feel unhappy now. If I change — reduce my resistance to change — I will feel even more unhappy." But the therapist persists, understanding that the stronger the resistance, the stronger the conflict. The treatment uses the keys of dreams and free associations to unlock these unconscious, repressed conflicts, which eventually emerge into consciousness and are worked out.

From his studies, Freud developed a new conception of

the structure of personality. He divided personality into three parts. The first, the **id** is the primitive part of the personality that the child brings into the world. The id is concerned only with self, and self-gratification is its only goal. With the id, emotions are uncensored and therefore expressed without inhibition.

When the outside world enters via the senses, some of the id is modified into a second (and primary) part of the personality, the **ego**. The ego is aware that the world comprises more than one's self alone and recognizes that in order to get along, compromises must be made despite the demands of the id. Freud compared the ego and the id to a rider and his horse. Usually, the rider can control the horse, but once in a while, the id bolts and runs away with the rider.

Finally, a third division, the **superego** develops. The superego is made up of the ideals and moral values provided to the child by parents, teachers, and other authority figures. Brill, stating that the superego is the highest mental evolution attainable by man, considers it "a precipitate of all prohibitions and inhibitions, all the rules of conduct which are impressed on the child by his parents and parent substitutes." When the superego is fully developed, it becomes the conscience, which guides us in differentiating right from wrong.

The **libido**, another Freudian concept, refers to the energy of the sexual instinct directed to an outside object. While this first was considered to be sexual in its narrowest sense, libido now is considered to represent the energy available for several kinds of love — sexual, self-love, love for parents and children, friendships, and almost any kind of strong attachment. Since no one knows how to measure this energy, the concept is difficult to understand; the same problem is encountered

with all conscious and unconscious functions of the mind, like
thoughts; how can we measure them? The libido theory considers development of the personality through a series of psy-
chosexual stages. Initially, the infant goes through an oral
phase where pleasure through ingestion is primary; later, an
anal stage, characterized by fascination with feces, replaces
the oral; finally, the genitals themselves become the centers
of gratification as the most mature stage of sexual development
is reached.

As stated earlier, psychoanalysis is but one of several forms
of psychotherapy and it is by no means the most common
one. The unique thing about the contributions of Freud and
the other early psychoanalysts was that their methods were
the first to open the previously locked doors to the unconscious where painful thoughts and feelings are buried.

Other Forms of Psychotherapy

Almost all forms of psychotherapy have one thing in common;
they attempt to discover the *causes* of emotional disturbances.
Thus, both clinical psychologists and physicians offer psychotherapy, using either psychoanalysis or one of the many other
techniques of therapy. (Psychology, originally confined to the
study of consciousness and behavior in humans and animals,
has grown in scope and now, along with medicine, includes
treatment of emotional disorders.)

In traditional psychoanalysis, the patient lies on a couch
and the therapist sits out of sight, allowing the patient to free
associate without distraction. The psychoanalyst rarely directs
the therapy. It is the patient who talks freely and through free

association of ideas, memories, and feelings, achieves **insight** (understanding) into the roots of the troublesome symptoms.

But only a minority of psychiatrists and psychologists use psychoanalysis. Instead, psychiatrists employ the most common form of psychotherapy — a discussion format — in which they take a more active role than do analysts. With this method, the therapist and patient sit facing each other and discuss the problems for which the patient has requested help. The therapist frequently asks questions (either to receive or impart information) and sometimes offers interpretations. Usually, some psychoanalytic techniques, such as dream interpretation, are used in addition to ordinary discussion. In addition, drugs that combat anxiety and depression sometimes are used to supplement psychotherapy. (For hospitalized patients, the use of drugs for severe depression has largely supplanted the older electroconvulsive therapy that was used to reverse the depression; this treatment consisted of a series of electric shock treatments producing short periods of unconsciousness.)

To accomplish the psychotherapeutic goal, a cooperative relationship between patient and therapist is fundamental. Working together, they uncover inner conflicts, which then are explored, discussed, and understood. Once understood, these conflicts that cause emotional pain are resolved, often giving the patient a sense of freedom never before experienced.

Although psychotherapy deals with serious mental disorders called **psychoses**, in which patients have a distorted view of reality and therefore often require institutional care, the bulk of treatment provided today by psychiatrists, clinical psychologists and trained social workers deals with patients with far less serious emotional problems. These lesser emotional problems called **psychoneuroses** are disturbances in which repression of painful thoughts results in the appearance of symptoms, prompting the patient to seek help. The word *psychoneurosis* is usually shortened to *neurosis*, and patients with neuroses are called neurotics. As commonly used, *neurotic* describes a nervous person, but the medical meaning is broader than his everyday usage. A neurotic patient may show no external signs of nervousness; however, anxiety is always present. Although neurotics may be hospitalized for an acute flare-up of their emotional problems, in the majority of instances treatment is conducted outside of a hospital on an outpatient basis.

Excepting those persons ordered by the courts to get psychiatric treatment and excepting the situations of unhappy children taken to psychiatrists by their parents, people seek psychotherapy voluntarily. Those who do so believe that the distress caused by their emotional problems can be eased or eliminated by treatment. Seeking this type of help is a sign neither of strength nor of weakness. It is a matter of personal philosophy. Many people go through life working out their own problems, or at least adjusting to them. Others feel that the help psychotherapy offers is worth the investment of time and money.

Until now, we have been talking about individual therapy; in recent years, however, group therapy has become popular and has proven highly effective. Group therapy is less expensive and offers the advantage of obtaining reactions from others in the group. Typically, a group consists of from five to eight members directed by the group leader, a therapist, and in this supportive atmosphere, through discussion, members of the group gain understanding of their problems as well as perspective, because they see that they are not unique in feeling inadequate at times. The feeling that everyone is in the same boat dispels the sense of isolation that frequently is present during unhappy periods.

A different type of group therapy, psychodrama, is often used in hospital therapy. In psychodrama, patients participate as actors in a play, unburdening their emotional problems to an audience of fellow patients and therapists who also may participate in the "play." This "acting out," along with the discussion that follows, frequently yields insights.

Because the emotional problems of children are being recognized earlier and because those treating these problems need to have special knowledge about the critical phases of child development, the specialty of child psychiatry has become a very important division of psychotherapy. The many forces shaping personality are especially active during the childhood years and during adolescence and because of the rapid changes taking place, these years can be particularly difficult and turbulent.

Essentially, child psychiatry is group psychiatry. In this type of treatment, the group is small, usually consisting of the child, parents, and therapist. Occasionally other family members participate. Parents are needed to give information; moreover, in many instances they have played a role in creating the child's emotional problems. With adolescents, the therapist may decide that it is important for the adolescent to work out his or her problems independent of parents; in these instances, the parents do not participate in treatment. The same judgment is occasionally made in the treatment of certain younger children. (On the basis of initial discussions and considering the child's attitude, the therapist makes the decision about individual vs. family therapy.) Teachers, social workers, and school psychologists often provide information to the therapist that supplements that given by parents.

The forms of treatment discussed in this chapter involve long discussions and frequently involve considerable expense. Many investigators feel that there are more direct approaches to emotional problems. There are numerous direct methods that attempt to relieve emotional stress and aim to help people to live fulfilled lives. Some of these methods or schools of thought are scientific, whereas others are led by untrained instructors. Currently, one of the most popular forms of emotional relaxation is one derived from Indian philosophy called TM (**transcendental meditation**); those practicing TM achieve tranquility by meditating several times a day while silently repeating a word called a *mantra*, which has been assigned to the person by a TM instructor. But of all the forms of "direct" therapy, behavior modification has the widest application and has been studied the most.

ELEVEN

Behavior Modification

The field of psychology known as behaviorism was born abruptly in 1913 when a 35-year-old investigator named John Broadus Watson announced that the goal of psychology was "the prediction and control of **behavior**." He proceeded to state boldly and unequivocally that "the time seems to have come when psychology must discard all references to consciousness; when it need no longer delude itself into thinking that it is making of mental states the object of observation."

This message was essentially a declaration of independence from the established fields of psychotherapy. Because consciousness, which includes thoughts and subjective feelings, can't be measured, Watson believed that psychoanalysis and the like were hocus pocus sciences and their results couldn't be verified. Therefore, he suggested, stick to what can be measured: overt behavior. How animals and people react to known stimuli is observable and measurable. Watson told his psychology brethren, many of whom disagreed with his concepts, that they should get back to the laboratory and study behavior by stimulus-response methods (S-R) similar to those responses discovered by Pavlov (*see* Chapter 4).

Just as Pavlov conditioned a dog to salivate not only when

food was presented but also when a bell was rung or when the footsteps of the attendant bringing food were heard, so too did Watson use his stimulus-response methods to alter the behavior of a small child. This child, "Little Albert," initially happily played with a white rat. Then, while the child was playing with the rat, Watson startled him by introducing a loud noise, and eventually the association of this unpleasant noise stimulus caused Albert to fear not only the white rat but almost anything furry. Like Pavlov, Watson had altered behavior by using new environmental stimuli.

Behaviorism attracted many new advocates, the most well-known being B.F. Skinner. Like Watson, Skinner believed that behavior could be modified (changed) by appropriate stimuli and that "good" behavior automatically will result from "good" stimuli originating from an ideal environment. In fact, Skinner, one of the originators of clinical behavior modification, described such an environment. In his 1948 book, *Walden II*, Skinner proposed a theoretical community where, by use of behavioral techniques, life would be happy for all, work would be reduced to four hours a day, much time would be spent on enjoyable and creative efforts, and discord would be eliminated. All of these ideal features would be perpetuated because the behavior of children growing up in this community would be ideally conditioned. Life indeed would be pleasant if everyone behaved in a manner that satisfied both individual and community goals, and indeed, some success has been reported in a small, cooperative college-living arrangement; however, a crime-free, joyous, creative, and productive full-scale Walden II community remains but a hope for the future.

The original behaviorist principles of Watson have been modified so that today most behaviorists do consider that conscious and unconscious thoughts and feelings, even though unmeasurable, are important.

Behavior modification emphasizes *learning* as its primary process in effecting change. Destructive habits, rather than being considered as unalterable, are viewed instead as behavior that can be reversed. Traditional psychotherapy uses verbal means to arrive at understanding problems and thereby change attitudes and feelings. Behaviorists believe in actively changing behavior first, with the knowledge that improvements in attitudes and feelings will follow. But it is obvious that any successful psychotherapy requires both thought and action. Freud himself recognized that fact. "One can hardly ever master a phobia," he declared, "if one waits till the patient lets the analysis influence him to give it up. . . . One succeeds only when one can induce them . . . to go about alone and to struggle with their anxiety while they make the attempt."

Positive reinforcement and extinction is the most common technique used for behavior modification. This method relies heavily on rewards for "good" behavior. This is because rewards reinforce and encourage repetition of this emerging "good" behavior. At the same time, unwanted behavior is diminished and on its way to becoming extinct through the process of taking away what is known as "secondary gain." At first glance, it seems silly that someone would gain something from behavior that results in criticism and disapproval. But a person exhibiting such behavior almost always gains attention, and when this unwanted behavior fails to bring forth the attention it used to elicit, it begins to disappear. So with positive reinforcement and extinction, the "good" behavior is rewarded while simultaneously "bad" behavior is punished. This

process is called **operant conditioning** because the environment "operates" on the behavior, conditioning and modifying
it.

Let's look at an example of behavior modification in the
classroom. A teacher we'll call Ms. Jones notices at the beginning of the school year that one boy in the class, Fred,
constantly talks to his neighbors and interrupts other pupils
when they're answering Ms. Jones's questions. When he is
called upon to give an answer he doesn't know, he responds
with wisecracks. During the previous year, the boy got away
with this behavior and although his grades were poor, his
former teacher passed him in self-defense. She didn't want
him back in her grade for a second year. Now Ms. Jones
analyzes the situation and decides that for the sake of Fred
as well as for the good of the class, this behavior is undesirable.
First she defines the behavior that needs to be changed. That's
easy — talking, interruptions, lack of preparation, and wisecracks. Also, she has a good idea of what this boy up to now
has gained from his behavior. She knows, because his former
teacher warned her, that the talking and interruptions have
resulted in a lot of threats about discipline and even a few
trips to the principal's office. So the boy has gained attention
for one thing. The other students laugh at his wisecracks, so
in addition to attention, he has gained (or thought he had
gained) approval from his peers. Ms. Jones has learned also
that the boy comes from a broken home, that no father is
present, and that his mother has no time for him. She now
approaches the situation differently from the previous teacher.
When Fred interrupts, Ms. Jones quietly tells him to stop
talking, but she doesn't give him a long public lecture. Fred
senses from her manner that she will not be the pushover his

earlier teacher was. After the first few days, Ms. Jones asks Fred to stay after class and explains what she has observed and what she expects. When next she calls on him and he is still unprepared and makes wisecracks, she quickly calls on someone else, and for the next few days she doesn't call on Fred at all. He understands that his lack of preparation hasn't helped him at all. Ms. Jones won't call on him now unless he has some idea of the answer, so he no longer has the pleasure of wisecracking and getting laughs. He'll get more attention from studying.

The next day when Ms. Jones asks a question, Fred knows the answer and to his classmates' amazement, he raises his hand and answers correctly. Ms. Jones is pleased and tells him so; his classmates actually are impressed; before when they laughed at him, they were laughing at a clown; Fred, an intelligent boy, suddenly realizes this. The approval of Ms. Jones and of his classmates acts as positive reinforcers, and the good feeling he gets from this approval encourages more cooperative behavior. In addition, Ms. Jones makes the unusual effort of going to Fred's home to talk to his mother, who has refused to come in to school for a conference. She manages to impress on Fred's mother, a harassed and worried wage earner, the fact that while Fred's schoolwork is improving, he needs attention and encouragement at home. Fred's mother confesses that she was unaware of how little attention she was giving her son and promises that she will try hard to make the home atmosphere better.

While obviously the above example is greatly oversimplified, the principles are sound. Timely rewards of approval reinforce desired behavior, and failure to continue to get reinforcement of undesirable behavior begins to extinguish that behavior. One further important fact should be noted: society itself tends to reinforce "normal" rather than "abnormal" behavior.

Actually, a system of positive reinforcements called the **token economy** has been used in hospitals, schools, prisons, and in the U.S. Army to modify behavior. The tokens (often small, metal, coinlike objects) are symbols used in the place of some other reward that can't be easily given on the spot. They are exchangeable later and can be anything that substitutes for a desired commodity or privilege, like access to a television set in a prison or commissary purchases in the Army. In some classrooms, the tokens are "points," which can be accumulated and used later to acquire a prize. Because tokens are awarded right at the time of a good behavior incident, there is immediate pleasurable association and so the desired behavior is reinforced.

An actual experiment in a state mental hospital first showed the value of a token economy. In that institution, there were many patients who, despite staff efforts, simply sat aimlessly doing nothing. The physicians and psychologists in charge decided to begin to reward desirable behavior with tokens. Desirable behavior was defined as the sort of activities — washing dishes, making beds, general housework — that had been done by attendants previously but that would be needed for the daily life of those patients who could eventually be discharged. The token rewards produced immediate success and in fact, patients selected the least desirable jobs because these jobs were rewarded with more tokens.

With situations like this experiment, it is absolutely necessary to have an ethics committee protect powerless patients by deciding if behavior modification experiments are morally right and in the best interests of these patients. Otherwise, the process becomes **brainwashing**, the worst sort of behavior modification. In brainwashing, which takes from one to four years, the will and ideals are broken by cruel and persistent psychological methods. These include persuasion by use of punishments like isolation and beatings, along with rewards such as increased food and more privileges.

Positive reinforcement has been used in many different situations. As an example of its use in reducing fear, consider the case of a woman who was terrified of travel on buses. At first, her therapy consisted of short bus trips during which the woman was accompanied by the therapist. After the short trips no longer frightened her, they were lengthened into longer rides. Finally, the woman had achieved enough confidence to try taking very short bus trips alone, and gradually, she was able to overcome her fear entirely. Important in the therapy was the fact that every improvement along the way was reinforced by appropriate praise, which motivated her continued improvement.

Biofeedback is an interesting type of behavior modification that depends on learning to counteract certain autonomic reactions to emotional stress. Actually, some of the most interesting and fundamental brain research deals with the autonomic nervous system, so named because it was supposed to act independently of will, in an involuntary or automatic fashion. Recent research proves that the autonomic nervous system has been incorrectly named; to the surprise of all except the imaginative researchers, it can be controlled by conscious thought, using training methods. For example, yogis in India

and elsewhere for years were considered to have a great deal
of control over breathing processes, and it was believed that
this was accomplished by some mystical means.

A few years ago, researchers in India asked one of the best-
known yoga practitioners to volunteer for a laboratory experiment. They placed the yogi in an airtight metal box that
contained instruments for measuring oxygen and carbon dioxide concentration. The yogi meditated before he was placed
in the box and attached to the instruments and he continued
to meditate during the course of the experiment. To the
amazement of the researchers, the yogi was able to remain
in the airtight box for several hours because he was able to
control the rate at which he burned oxygen. He consumed
far less of this vital gas than the scientists had believed possible.

Professor Neal Miller, of Rockefeller University in New
York City, began the studies that showed that higher brain
centers could be used to teach control of autonomic functions.
The process used is one of biofeedback, a word that means
exactly what it says — information about biological processes,
such as blood pressure state or heart rate, is "fed back" to an
experimental subject so that he or she can tell what is happening. The feedback is accomplished by visual or auditory
instruments; the subject can see on a screen or hear by use
of various tones or other sounds the direction of biological
change. For example, if a girl is hooked up to a blood pressure
machine, which in turn is connected to a sound transmitter,
she can learn how to lower or raise her blood pressure, a
process thought to be impossible only a few decades ago.
When she relaxes properly, the blood pressure begins to drop
and a beeping sound tells her that she is responding properly.

The aim is to train her so that in time she will not require a machine to cue her.

Essentially, the instruments used in biofeedback record the effect of emotional response in the same way that a lie detector does. Just as the emotional strain of telling a lie increases heart rate, causes sweating, and changes breathing and blood pressure patterns, so too do stress-related diseases. But in biofeedback, the stressful physiological changes are *shown* to the patient as part of the process of teaching relaxation so as to avoid these changes.

Biofeedback has been used in the treatment of hypertension, asthma, migraine headaches, and several other disorders. It rarely is used as the primary or sole method of treatment because in severe types of elevated blood pressure, for example, medication is more effective. Furthermore, no one is certain if the effects of biofeedback training are long-lasting. The investigational and therapeutic work that is underway will, however, provide much new information about this fascinating science.

There are a few other techniques of behavior modification besides the primary ones just discussed. One of these is **aversion therapy**. This technique uses stimuli that create unpleasant associations with the undesirable behavior. Rather than accentuating the positive, as the most successful behavior modification techniques do, aversion uses punishment.

An example of this would be the case of an alcoholic who wants to quit. In a sanitarium, he is told that liquor is unhealthy for the body and that experiments will prove this. He is then given an ounce of whiskey to smell, taste, enjoy, and drink; then he is given an injection that in a short while produces vomiting. Usually, several of these "treatments" are given over a ten-day period. Liquor now is associated with the very unpleasant sensation of nausea and vomiting. One study reports a 50 percent cure rate from this treatment.

Another type of aversion therapy involves unpleasant verbal or visual stimuli. For example, an obese person who should avoid high-calorie foods might be shown a movie in which these rich foods are shown with worms crawling around and through them.

Aversion therapy seems to work for a while but in most cases, its effects wear off quickly. In general, other behavior modification techniques show better results so that today, aversion therapy is used much less frequently than it once was.

Another behavior modication technique is called **flooding**. In this case, the patient is persuaded to deal with a feared situation, not by avoiding it, but rather by either imagining it as vividly as possible or by directly confronting it for various periods of time. By deliberately provoking anxiety on several occasions for varying periods of time, investigators have succeeded in having volunteer subjects realize that the situation they had been avoiding out of fear wasn't really so frightening after all. Flooding is based on habituation, a term that simply means getting used to something. When a situation becomes familiar, its dimensions are known and the terror it evoked before no longer is present.

Behavior modification has been used successfully to effect personality changes in the Type A individuals discussed in Chapter 9. Groups of Type A individuals have learned to be less time conscious, to wait patiently in lines rather than fuming, to listen quietly to others rather than interrupting impatiently, and generally to become happier and more relaxed.

Annoyance, impatience, anger, and irritation are classic qualities of Type A individuals and these are the emotions that are worked on, largely by means of self-monitoring. The incidence of heart attacks has been greatly reduced in these individuals by teaching them to relax, and now a Type A Intervention Program is in effect at the United States Army War College.

The successful treatment of alcoholism is one of the most dramatic examples of behavior modification. Psychiatric treatment does little good while a person continues to drink and psychiatric treatment is not effective in making alcoholics stop drinking. Action, not words, is required. The alcoholic must simply decide to stop, and most often an organization like AA (Alcoholics Anonymous) will provide badly needed support during the immediate postdrinking period and later as well. And from the time that the critical decision to stop drinking has been made, behavior is modified in the most constructive way.

As mentioned earlier, in behavior modification, a person has the ability to monitor his or her own improvement and recognize what is being accomplished. When an individual is able to acknowledge the courage and persistence it took to overcome an undesired behavior and give himself or herself several pats on the back, he or she is giving the best type of reinforcement. Few things are more satisfying than awareness that self-control has been responsible for effective action.

TWELVE

Personality Tests

For generations, tests of all sorts have been used to get information quickly. Intelligence, aptitude for various occupations, and personality are among the most frequent qualities measured. Personality assessment, in particular, helps in diagnosis of both normal and abnormal emotional responses and in the treatment of abnormalities.

Personality, the sum total of emotional trends that result in an individual and recognizable behavior pattern, is a unique quality. While we easily recognize outgoing, happy personalities, we are also able to distinguish innumerable individual differences in this broad group, just as there are differences among those classified as withdrawn. Assessment by testing gives information that is useful not only to the behavioral psychologist but to all clinical psychologists and psychiatrists.

There are two main techniques of **personality assessment testing**, projective and objective. The projective tests employ very ambiguous, unclear stimuli, and the responses show more unconscious aspects of personality. Therefore, the projective tests elicit and reveal a subtle and shaded version of one's inner feelings and conflicts. The objective tests, on the other hand, offer clear, definite stimuli in the form of unambiguous, direct questions that are answered by those persons taking the tests. We will briefly discuss the most popular test in each category — the projective **Rorschach** inkblot test and the objective **Minnesota Multiphasic Personality Inventory**, better known as the MMPI.

Hermann Rorschach, a Swiss psychiatrist, developed a series of ten inkblots that he felt would help the clinician to uncover and understand unconscious factors of personality. Some of the inkblots were black and white, some employed shading, and five used colors, red or pastels. Unfortunately, Rorschach never had a chance to develop a systematic key to interpreting these inkblots because he died in 1922 at the age of 38.

The method of scoring the responses to the inkblots frequently varies with the person giving the test, although certain standard ways of scoring have been developed. Actually, many professionals do not score the results at all but from the responses draw intuitive inferences about the subject's personality.

The test is administered by presenting each of the inkblots in order and asking the subject to tell what each one looks like or might be. Depending on what the person being tested "sees" in the inkblots, the examiner (if there is no dependence on a standardized scoring system) looks at the content of the responses and then makes certain conclusions. If the inkblot looks like a butterfly but the person being tested sees violent scenes like the arms of a person being twisted by someone or if the center of the "butterfly" appears to be a body whose head has been torn off, the examiner may draw a common-sense conclusion that the person is hostile and aggressive or that the person is insecure and frightened by his or her environment. But if, instead of this seat-of-the-pants interpretation, such features as how much of the inkblot is used, how common (popular) are the responses, how much movement is seen, how much color figures in the response, how many total responses are given to each inkblot, etc., then the result is a standardized scoring for various categories of personality.

Because of the great variability in interpretation of responses, the Rorschach is considered an unreliable test, at least on any quantitative basis. Other projective tests include the thematic apperception test (TAT) in which the person being tested responds to a series of pictures by telling a story about what the picture represents, thus providing insight into feelings; the draw-a-person (DAP) test where subjects draw male and female figures and describe the personalities of these figures; and the incomplete sentences blank (ISB) in which the subject completes an incomplete sentence like "I feel . . . ."

As there are many projective tests such as the ones listed above, so too are there several objective personality assessment tests. The most popular of these, the Minnesota Multiphasic Personality Inventory (MMPI), was developed in the late 1930's and early 1940's by a psychologist-psychiatrist team working at the University of Minnesota Hospitals. Drs. S. R. Hathaway and J. C. McKinley hoped that the test they had devised would be an efficient and reliable way of arriving at psychiatric diagnoses, and indeed, today it is the most widely used and heavily researched personality inventory. Although younger subjects have taken the MMPI, it is suggested that subjects be 16 years old or older and have a reading level of at least sixth grade.

The test consists of 550 questions about one's feelings, which can be answered either by "true," "false," or "cannot say." The average time required to complete the test is approximately an hour and a half, and the answers to the questions determine to what extent each of ten selected qualities or emotional problems (called scales) is present. These include depression, hypochondriasis (too much concern and worry about physical ailments), male-female attributes, and seven other categories contributing to personality. There are ways to determine how honestly the questions are being answered and to determine if a person is faking in order to create a good impression or even faking with the purpose of creating a false impression of being more disturbed than is the case.

The questions that Hathaway and McKinley selected for the test, as well as their interpretation of the answers given and subsequent scoring, depend on common sense. For example, certain feelings are known to be associated with depression — feeling sad most of the day, feeling unworthy, waking up at four or five each morning feeling blue and anxious, losing one's appetite, etc. — and if the person scores high with many "yes" answers to questions about feeling unhappy and having a low self-esteem, obviously depression is present, assuming the person has answered honestly.

Although no test is completely reliable, most investigators feel that the MMPI has significant value in identifying emotional trouble spots and in suggesting the direction of psychological treatment when such treatment is indicated.

There are many objective personality assessment tests besides the MMPI, including the Edwards Personal Preference Schedule, California Psychological Inventory, Mooney Problem Check List, and Sixteen Personality Factor Questionnaire. Each one has its advocates and as there is no definitive answer as to which test is the most reliable or reproducible, research into testing continues; these tests and others are constantly being refined and improved.

Although many of these tests have been given to adolescents of 15 and even 14 years old, they are considered inappropriate for children any younger. One problem is reading level and another is content. Questions about the subject's sex life, for example, would have little meaning to a prepubescent child. Accordingly, useful personality inventories suitable for younger children have been developed. The first of these, the Missouri Children's Picture Series (MCPS) is used with children from ages 5 to 16. The test uses a series of line drawings of children playing games, skating, and generally doing things that young people find pleasurable. There are 238 of these drawings printed on small cards, which the children being tested look at. Then they place each card either into a "like" pile if the activity appeals to them or into a "dislike" pile if it doesn't. The responses, which give clues to the child's personality, are then evaluated.

The Personality Inventory for Children (PIC) is an assessment test for even younger children (age three and up). This test has a format similar to the MMPI except that in this case, the parents respond to various statements that they believe either apply or don't apply to their child. Then, like other objective tests, the PIC is scored for various qualities such as Achievement, Intellectual Screening, Development, Somatic Concern (same as hypochondriasis), Depression, Family Relations, and some 22 other categories. PIC is considered by experts to be highly reliable and likely to be used increasingly in the future.

THIRTEEN

Emotional Health

As we have discovered, emotional maturity is achieved gradually. Piaget pointed out that emotional growth is related to age. As we grow up to and through adolescence, we reach each stage of emotional growth until finally we achieve full emotional maturity. Wise and understanding parents can influence a child's emotional development but the fact remains that each of us is genetically unique and each has the independent capacity to learn and grow emotionally. We have the ability to chart our own lives.

Despite our individual differences, there are some facts about emotional health that apply to all of us because we have many things in common. We all have similar physical characteristics (organ systems) and we experience the same emotions. Because of these similarities, we are able to communicate with each other and reach understanding.

Man probably developed the ability to walk upright some four million years ago because it freed his hands for carrying food and other items that could be shared. There was a biological advantage to walking upright. From his beginnings, man learned that cooperation was beneficial and better than functioning alone most of the time.

General Principles of Emotional Health

1. "Know thyself," the advice inscribed at the Delphic oracle, is a cardinal rule in learning to tell when an emotional response is appropriate. To know ourselves, we must have the courage to examine how we *really* feel — not how we *should* feel — about the people and situations we encounter in day to day living.

2. We can work on those parts of our personality we wish to improve. We are adaptable. Every month, there are articles in childrens', teen, and adult magazines that counsel about emotional problems and emotional growth, and many books in the same field have been written. All of this advice would be useless were it not for one basic truth: If we want to, we have the ability to change our behavior.

3. We should express feelings instead of bottling them up. Even when we refrain from letting the outside world know what we are feeling, we can at least express our feelings silently to ourselves. Emotions are not controlled by denial; although they are not allowed to surface, they are there, dammed up and doing damage.

4. We should avoid the trap of generalizing from a specific failure into a general feeling of failure. Achievement is rarely "all or nothing at all." For example, a boy who doesn't make the varsity football team may incorrectly conclude that he's a poor athlete. Maybe he didn't train hard enough or maybe he's not big enough or maybe he's simply not as good at football as the ones who made the team, but he runs well and he plays tennis well. Some people make the unreasonable assumption that if they're not perfect, then they're bad.

5. We can maintain perspective about the stresses we are dealing with by understanding them. Today, people in authority frequently want to know how we handle pressure. The stress interview developed for this purpose is used by some colleges for interviewing applicants and also is used by prospective employers as a job-screening technique. To determine how well a person will react under pressure, the interviewer in such a session will try to unnerve the person being interviewed. Often, questions that present difficult moral conflicts and therefore elicit strong emotional responses are asked. ("If you worked for a bank and you had inside information that it was going to fail, would you tell family members to take their money out of the bank?")

Knowing yourself and your moral values makes it possible to answer thorny questions like these honestly. Sometimes, an "I don't know" is the only response possible.

6. When we feel love or friendship, touching and being touched is emotionally healthy. We know that adequately fed infants who are deprived of loving touch (holding, kissing, hugging, caressing, massaging, etc.) fail to thrive and sometimes die as a result of this sort of neglect. It is a biological truth that primates need physical contact during emotional stress; experiments in the wild have shown that baboons, when suddenly presented with great danger, cling to one another. Touch is important for all humans.

7. The habit of positive thinking results in a feeling of well-being. When we think and communicate actively instead of being a passive recipient of thoughts that lower self-esteem, we are happier. This requires the discipline of thinking of ourselves as individuals instead of allowing the outside world

(such as TV commercials) to tell us what we should be. Positive thinking requires active and continuous work until it becomes a habit. An article in the *American Journal of Nursing* suggests using the word *but* to start on the road to positive thinking. The author advises that when a negative emotion is felt or stated, it should be amended to end on a positive note. "I did poorly in school today, *but* I did well yesterday and I'll do better tomorrow." Eventually, the totally negative thoughts will decrease in frequency.

Positive actions and expression help to develop the habit of positive thinking when negative thoughts are present. It is a truth that if we force ourselves to smile despite feeling unhappy, we'll begin to feel happier. If a person wants to feel confident, he or she should start to act confident.

8. Exercise, particularly aerobic exercise, which gives the heart and other organs a workout, has been proven to make us feel better. Because muscular exertion is an antidote to depression, a program that includes exercise, such as jogging, calisthenics, or swimming, should be performed routinely unless there is medical advice to the contrary.

9. We can relieve worrisome physical and emotional problems by discussing them with parents, family physicians, psychologists, school counselors, clergymen, or others. A variety of moods is normal. While understandably we prefer to feel good, we all experience unhappy times and occasions when we feel anxious or angry. (Many psychiatrists feel that anger itself, when repressed, causes depression.)

When we experience excessive or prolonged unhappiness (beyond four to six weeks), it is advisable to seek professional help to root out the cause of the depression.

Thoughts of suicide that everyone has from time to time may accompany prolonged depression. It is a myth that discussion of suicide will cause it to happen. The reverse is true. If these thoughts are present, honest discussion of the stresses that caused them will provide relief. For those who feel too uncomfortable talking about this to one's family or family doctor, almost every community has hospital psychiatric emergency clinics or mental health outpatient clinics where help is available. Also, many cities have Suicide Prevention Centers and Crisis Centers where trained volunteers will give advice over the telephone and the caller need not give his or her name.

10. We should avoid creating unhappiness for ourselves because we have set impossible standards. We're often too ambitious when we set our immediate goals, and these unreal expectations are discouraging. It's more intelligent to plan on step-by-step achievement rather than expecting to be immediately successful at an impossibly big project. We all can achieve little "wins," and eventually they will culminate in big wins.

11. We should not expect to be adult at all times. Many of the pleasures of childhood — play, freedom, the feeling of being protected, and so forth — remain with us throughout life; maturity consists of a healthy balance between these pleasures and the satisfaction derived from taking responsibility.

These are some of the important guidelines for maintaining emotional health. In earlier chapters, we became familiar with the history of emotions, with the wide variety of emotions and with their physical and psychological functions. We have learned how emotions are expressed and how some illnesses occur when emotions work against us. We have discussed the broad field of psychotherapy and have become acquainted with the most frequently used psychological tests. Finally, we understand that we have the power to control our emotions so that they work *for* us, not against us.

Glossary

ACNE. A universal skin disorder affecting adolescents caused by oversecretion of the fatty lubricating material, sebum, along with plugging of the ducts of the sebaceous glands adjoining hair follicles that produce sebum.

ADAPTATION. Adjustment to a new set of conditions.

ADOLESCENCE. The period of time, beginning with puberty, during which the child matures into an adult. Because it is characterized by rapid physical, intellectual, and emotional growth, adolescence is almost always turbulent. During this period, Piaget's "formal operations" thinking emerges and with it, the ability to think abstractly.

ADRENAL GLANDS. Paired glands, located above the kidneys, which control the salt-and-water balance of the body. In addition to controlling salt and water, they also produce hormones that reduce inflammation, hormones that are important for sexual development, and adrenaline, the powerful hormone secreted under conditions of great stress.

ALCOHOLISM. The disease caused by an addiction to alcohol.

ALIENATION. The lonely process of progressive withdrawal from family and friends; when it occurs, it does so under conditions of extreme emotional strain.

ANGER. A strong feeling of displeasure and usually of antagonism.

ANGINA PECTORIS. A squeezing type of chest pain associated with coronary artery disease and often precipitated by emotion.

121

ANOREXIA NERVOSA. A disease of female adolescence, characterized by a rapid loss of weight caused by extreme dieting in a
young person who has become obsessed by the concept that she
is overweight.

ANTICIPATION. Advance thought. Commonly refers to looking forward with pleasure (or displeasure) to something that will occur
at some future time.

ANXIETY. A feeling of strong or dominating blend of uncertainty,
agitation or dread, and brooding fear about some contingency;
the fear that something *may* happen that will hurt us. Pervasive
uneasiness without conscious knowledge of what is causing it is
called free-floating anxiety.

ASTHMA. The most common chronic lung disorder of adolescents,
characterized by difficult and wheezing respiration caused by spasm
of the bronchial airways (especially the bronchioles) and the excessive production of mucus, which also obstructs the passage of air.

AVERSION THERAPY. A behavior modification technique that uses
unpleasant stimuli to create unpleasant associations with the undesirable behavior.

BEHAVIOR. The way of conducting oneself in society.

BEHAVIOR MODIFICATION. A method of changing undesirable
behavior into desirable behavior. Using positive and negative
reinforcement to create the desired behavioral associations, the
technique emphasizes learning as its primary process in effecting
change.

BIOFEEDBACK. A behavior-modification technique that provides
information about biological processes, such as blood pressure
state or heart rate, by "feeding back" the monitored information
to the patient so that he or she can tell what is happening. The
feedback is accomplished by visual or auditory instruments.

BODY LANGUAGE. The nonverbal expression of emotion, either
conscious (when we purposely show a facial expression or gesture)
or unconscious (when we are unaware that we have made a nonverbal response); all nonverbal communication really is saying in
actions what we either consciously or unconsciously want to express in words.

BRAINWASHING. Behavior modification during which the will and ideals are broken by cruel and persistent psychological methods, including persuasion by use of punishments and rewards.

BULIMIA. A disorder closely associated with anorexia nervosa, characterized by periodic binge eating.

CATHARSIS. The psychological process of bringing painful buried conflicts to the surface, as a result of the patient's free associations and discussions of problems and dreams during the course of psychiatric treatment.

COLITIS. Bowel inflammation with associated diarrhea.

CONDITIONED REFLEX. A trained physiological response to an unnatural stimulus. For example, a dog normally salivates at the sight of food but not when a bell is rung; however, if a bell is repeatedly rung at the same time as food is presented, eventually, even in the absence of food, the dog will salivate when the bell sounds because now it associates the sound with food.

CONFLICTS. Thoughts or feelings that pull in opposite directions, resulting in anxiety.

CORONARY ARTERY DISEASE. The type of heart disease resulting from the plugging of the blood vessels that nourish the heart itself, caused by deposits of cholesterol and other fatty substances in combination with calcium.

DEPRESSION. A prolonged state of sadness, lasting well beyond what is appropriate for the situation that precipitated it.

DESIRE. The conscious impulse toward an object or experience that promises enjoyment or satisfaction in its attainment.

DETERMINATION. The ability to persist against opposition or attempts to dissuade or discourage; one of the most important positive emotions because it implies that the person believes that she or he, as an individual, has effective power and therefore accepts the challenge to accomplish some aim.

DISGUST. The physical or emotional reaction comparable to nausea that is excited by exposure to something highly distasteful or loathsome.

EGO. The part of the personality that results from modification of the id and is aware that the world comprises more than one's self alone; the ego recognizes that in order to get along, compromises must be made despite the undisciplined demands of the id.

EMBARRASSMENT. A state of self-conscious distress caused by certain situations or by the actions of a person or persons.

EMOTION. A departure from the normal calm state of an organism of such nature as to include strong feeling, an impulse toward open action, and certain internal physical reactions; any one of the states designated as fear, anger, love, hate, desire, disgust, grief, joy, surprise, etc.

ENDOCRINE SYSTEM. The system comprising glands that manufacture and secrete hormones directly into the bloodstream.

ENVY. Painful or resentful awareness of the advantage enjoyed by another, accompanied by a desire to possess the same advantage.

ENZYMES. Organic substances that speed chemical transformations in order to aid processes like digestion, respiration, etc.

EXPRESSION. Expressed emotions are made known to the outside world through either verbal or body language.

EXTROVERT. An outgoing person whose interests focus on objects and actions of the outside world.

FEAR. Agitated foreboding, often of some real or specific peril.

FIGHT OR FLIGHT. Cannon's famous theory, which states that perception of emotions mobilizes the autonomic nervous system, stimulating the adrenal glands to secrete adrenaline, preparing animals and humans for emergency action in dangerous situations.

FLOODING. A behavior modification technique that has a patient deal with a feared situation either by imagining it as vividly as possible or by directly confronting it, rather than by avoiding it.

FORMAL OPERATIONS. The final of Piaget's three stages of emotional and intellectual development, during which adolescents develop sufficient maturity to reflect about their thoughts, to form ideals and, because of advanced reasoning ability, to plan realistically for the future.

FREE ASSOCIATION. The process used in psychoanalysis whereby the patient relates to the psychiatrist every thought that spontaneously comes to mind.

GENERAL ADAPTATION SYNDROME. The body's defense against acute and chronic stress described by Selye and characterized by three phases: first, the alarm reaction when the adrenals enlarge, the lymph tissue shrinks, and stomach ulcerations occur; next, the stage of resistance, during which period the body attempts to defend itself against stress by actions of the nervous and endocrine systems; finally, the stage of exhaustion, when the body is worn out and requires rest.

GUILT. Feelings of culpability, especially for imagined offenses or from a sense of inadequacy: morbid self-reproach often manifest in marked preoccupation with the moral correctness of one's behavior.

HATE. A sustained feeling in which strong dislike is combined with ill will toward the hated object.

HEADACHE. Migraine is the type of stress headache caused by dilation of one of the external blood vessels of the head and usually involving one half of the head. Tension headache is the extremely common type of headache that occurs under stressful conditions requiring prolonged concentration and is caused by muscular contraction, usually involving the neck muscles.

HORMONES. Powerful chemical substances manufactured by endocrine glands and secreted directly into the bloodstream.

HOST RESISTANCE. The ability of the body to resist disease.

HYPERTENSION. High blood pressure.

HYPNOSIS. A state very close to normal sleep, created by concentration by the person being hypnotized on the commands of the hypnotist; used by therapists treating emotional problems as a method of releasing repressed memories from the minds of patients.

HYSTERIA. A condition, found mostly in women, where physical signs really are caused by emotional problems; for example, a patient might be unable to move her arm, but the paralysis is in her mind, and nothing is physically wrong with the arm.

ID. The primitive part of the personality that the child brings into the world, concerned only with self, with self-gratification its only goal; emotions are uncensored and therefore expressed without inhibition.

INSIGHT. The sudden understanding of a problem, usually following long discussion of the problem, when all at once, everything comes together and understanding is achieved.

INSTINCTS. The inherited patterns of behavior.

INTROVERT. A person who concentrates on inner thoughts and fantasies rather than on what is occurring in the outside world; because of this inwardness an introvert is more thoughtful and less outgoing than an extrovert.

JEALOUSY. The state in which one is intolerant of rivalry or unfaithfulness.

JOY. The feeling excited by the acquisition or expectation of good.

KINESICS. The modern science of body language in which subtle, unconscious expressions reveal one's emotional response.

LIBIDO. A Freudian concept, referring to the energy of the sexual instinct directed to an outside object; at first considered to be sexual in its narrowest sense, libido now is considered to represent the energy available for several kinds of love — sexual, self-love, love for parents and children, friendships, and almost any kind of strong attachment.

LOVE. The attraction, desire, or affection felt for a person who arouses delight or admiration or elicits tenderness, sympathetic interest, or benevolence.

MEMORY. Sensory experiences stored by the brain that can be recalled when needed.

MENARCHE. The time menstrual periods commence, usually occurring between the ages of 10½ and 16.

MIND. The total conscious and unconscious content of thoughts and feelings initiated by brain activity; most commonly used to refer to the intellectual output of the brain.

MINNESOTA MULTIPHASIC PERSONALITY INVENTORY (MMPI). The most popular objective personality assessment test, developed in late 1930's and early 1940's by a psychologist-psychiatrist team working at the University of Minnesota Hospitals, and consisting of 550 questions about one's feelings, which can be answered either by "true," "false," or "cannot say." The average time required to complete the test is approximately an hour and a half; answers to the questions determine to what extent each of ten selected qualities or emotional problems (scales) is present.

MOOD. A persistent emotional state. When someone feels and acts unhappy over a prolonged period of time, that person is said to be in a bad mood.

MOTOR PATHWAYS. The collections of nerves traveling from the brain that control muscular movement. *Motor* is another word for movement.

MYOCARDIAL INFARCTION. Another word for heart attack, an event that occurs when the heart's own blood vessels are severely plugged.

NERVOUS SYSTEM. The system comprising the brain, spinal cord, and all the nerves of the body and their connections. The nervous system receives and sends out the messages that control all the varied activities of our bodies. The *Central Nervous System (C.N.S.)* is the division of the nervous system that controls mental activity and *voluntary* physical activity. The *autonomic nervous system* is the division of the nervous system that controls involuntary activity of visceral organs, those such as the heart, stomach, intestines, etc.

OBESITY. Markedly excessive body weight.

OPERANT CONDITIONING. The process used in behavior modification that rewards desirable behavior and punishes undesirable behavior, so named because the environment "operates" on the behavior, conditioning and modifying it.

OVARIES. The paired female endocrine glands that produce the sex hormone estrogen, which affects sexual development, activity, and reproduction.

PANCREAS. The large gland that makes the hormone insulin, which controls the use of sugars by the body; also serves as an exocrine gland, secreting digestive enzymes through a duct into the bowel.

PARATHYROIDS. The four tiny endocrine glands, located inside or behind the thyroid, that control the calcium balance of the body.

PERSONALITY. The sum total of emotional trends that result in an individual and recognizable behavior pattern; although there are classes of personality such as "outgoing" or "introverted," each person's personality has unique features.

PERSONALITY ASSESSMENT TESTING. *Objective* tests offer clear, definite stimuli in the form of unambiguous, direct questions or statements. *Projective* tests employ very ambiguous, unclear stimuli, revealing the unconscious aspects of personality, the subtle and shaded versions of one's inner feelings and conflicts.

PITUITARY. The master endocrine gland, which secretes trophic (nutritive) hormones acting on the other endocrine glands and also secretes growth hormone.

PHYSIOLOGY. The study of the functions and activities of living matter that discovers the reason for *why* the various systems of the body, along with their component organs and tissues, do what they do as well as the study of *how* these systems work.

PROPRIOCEPTION. The position sense whose receptors in the nervous system relay information about exactly where in space the various parts of the body are positioned.

PSYCHIATRIST. A professional, usually a physician, specializing in the diagnosis and treatment of emotional disorders.

PSYCHOANALYSIS. The "talking cure," whereby painful, repressed memories are released, resulting in the relief of emotional distress; usually, the patient lies on a couch and remembers painful events with the help of the psychiatrist, who analyzes the meaning to the patient of these unhappy buried memories.

PSYCHOLOGIST. A professional, often a doctor of philosophy, who like a psychiatrist, specializes in the diagnosis and treatment of emotional disorders.

PSYCHONEUROSES. Disturbances in which repression of painful thoughts results in the appearance of symptoms, prompting the patient to seek help; usually shortened to *neurosis*, and patients with neuroses are called neurotics. Neurotic patients function within the real world, however poorly. (*See* psychoses.)

PSYCHOSES. Serious mental disorders in which patients have a distorted view of reality and often require institutional care.

PSYCHOSOMATIC DISEASE. One in which emotion significantly contributes to its cause.

PSYCHOTHERAPY. The specialty that deals with the treatment of emotional disorders.

PUBERTY. A period of rapid biological growth marking the start of adolescence (average age 10½ in females and 12 in males) when development of sex organs and secondary sexual characteristics, such as growth of axillary hair, begins.

RECEPTORS. Tiny cells located in the various sense organs, the first parts of the body to receive sensory messages of light, sound, heat, cold, etc., from the outside world; located inside organs and tissues.

REPRESSION. Blockage of an emotional response because the person isn't consciously aware of the situation provoking it.

RESISTANCE. A psychoanalytic term referring to a patient's efforts to prevent the releasing of painful, repressed conflicts.

RORSCHACH. The most popular of the projective personality assessment tests, consisting of a series of ten inkblots, which are presented to the patient; the responses as to what the patient "sees" in the ambiguous inkblots give clues to personality.

SENSES. Specialized mechanisms composed of connected nerve cells, which allow us to receive and respond to both external and internal stimuli.

SORROW. Uneasiness or anguish caused by loss (as of something loved or familiar).

STRESS. The rate of all the wear and tear caused by life; when referring to emotions, it means an unpleasant feeling of pressure.

SUPEREGO. That part of the personality made up of the ideals and moral values provided to the child by parents, teachers, and other authority figures; results in the formation of a conscience.

SUPPRESSION. Prevention of emotional response through conscious efforts.

SURPRISE. The state of being taken unaware without time for preparation.

SYNAPSES. The connections between nerve cells where chemicals are released to permit nerve impulses to be transmitted from one nerve cell to the next.

SYNDROME. A series of signs and symptoms that together constitute an illness.

TESTES. The paired male endocrine glands that produce the sex hormone testosterone, which affects sexual development, activity, and reproduction.

THYROID. The unpaired endocrine gland located in the neck that controls metabolism, the rate at which the body uses food.

TOKEN ECONOMY. A system of positive reinforcements used in hospitals, schools, prisons, and in the U.S. Army to modify behavior in which tokens are used in the place of some other reward that can't be easily given on the spot, to be exchanged later for the desired rewards.

TRANSCENDENTAL MEDITATION. A form of emotional relaxation derived from Indian philosophy and called TM; those practicing it achieve tranquility by meditating several times a day while silently repeating a word called a mantra.

TRANSFERENCE. A psychoanalytic term referring to a patient's transferring to the therapist the emotional attachments that existed in early life; essentially, the patient repeats the relationship he or she had with parents, feeling toward the therapist the same loves and hates as toward the parents while growing up.

ULCER, PEPTIC. The erosion of a portion of the lining of the stomach or first part of the small intestine (duodenum) produced when stress results in spasm and increased acid production.

Bibliography

Many of the references listed below are technical but appropriate for a reader who has some background in science. The starred references were written for a general readership.

Agras, W. S., *Behavior Modification*. Boston: Little, Brown & Co., 1972.

Arroyo, D., and Tonkin, R. "Adolescents with Bulimic and Non-bulimic Eating Disorders." *Journal of Adolescent Health Care*, 6(1): 21–4 Jan. 1985.

*Bruch, Hilde. *The Golden Cage*. Cambridge, Mass.: Harvard University Press, 1978.

*Cannon, Walter B. *Bodily Changes in Pain, Hunger, Fear and Rage*. New York: D. Appleton-Century Co., 1929.

Craighead, W. E., Kasdin, A. E., and Mahoney, M. J. *Behavior Modification*. Boston: Houghton Mifflin Co., 1976.

Cicchetti, D., and Hesse, P. *Emotional Development*. San Francisco: Jossey-Bass Inc., 1982.

*Darwin, Charles. *The Expression of the Emotions in Man and Animals*. 1872. Reprint. New York: Philosophical Library, 1955.

Elkind, David. *Children and Adolescents*. New York: Oxford University Press, 1981.

Erikson, Erik. *Childhood and Society*. New York: W.W. Norton & Co., 1950.

*Fast, Julius. *Body Language*. New York: Pocket Books, 1970.

Freud, Sigmund. *The Basic Writings of Sigmund Freud*. Translated by A. A. Brill. New York: Random House, Modern Library, 1938.

Graham, John R., and Lilly, Roy S. *Psychological Testing*. Englewood Cliffs, N.J.: Prentice-Hall Inc., 1984.

Guyton, Arthur C. *Human Physiology and Mechanisms of Disease*. Philadelphia: W.B. Saunders Co., 1982.

Hofmann, Adele. *Adolescent Medicine*. Reading, Mass.: Addison Wesley Publishing Co., 1983.

*Knapp, Mark L. *Nonverbal Communication in Human Interaction*. New York: Holt, Rinehart & Winston, 1978.

Knowles, Ruth D. "Disputing Irrational Thoughts," *American Journal of Nursing*, 81(4):735 April 1981.

Patterson, Miles L. *Nonverbal Behavior*. New York: Springer-Verlag, 1983.

Plutchik, R. and Kellerman, H., eds. *Emotion: Theory, Research and Experience*, vol. 1. New York: Academic Press, 1980.

*Ray, Marie B. *Doctors of the Mind*. Boston: Little, Brown & Co., 1946.

Robeck, Mildred C. *Infants and Children*. New York: McGraw-Hill Book Co., 1978.

Saul, Leon J. *Emotional Maturity*. Philadelphia: J.B. Lippincott Co., 1960.

*Selye, Hans. *The Stress of Life*. New York: McGraw-Hill Book Co., 1956.

Selye, Hans. *Stress in Health and Disease*. Boston/London: Butterworths, 1976.

Spence, Alexander P., and Mason, Elliot B. *Human Anatomy and Physiology*. Menlo Park: Benjamin/Cummings Publishing Group, 1983.

Watson, Robert I. *The Great Psychologists: from Aristotle to Freud*. Philadelphia: J.B. Lippincott Co., 1963.

Wolf, S., and Wolff, H. G. *Human Gastric Function*. New York: Oxford University Press, 1943.

*Wolff, H. G. *Stress and Disease*. Springfield, Ill.: Charles C. Thomas Publisher, 1968.

Index